CW00411373

William Shakespeare (bapt. 26 April 1564 – 23 April 1616) was an English poet, playwright and actor, widely regarded as the greatest writer in the English language and the world's greatest dramatist. He is often called England's national poet and the "Bard of Avon". His extant works, including collaborations, consist of approximately 39 plays, 154 sonnets, two long narrative poems, and a few other verses, some of uncertain authorship. His plays have been translated into every major living language and are performed more often than those of any other playwright. Shakespeare was born and raised in Stratford-upon-Avon, Warwickshire. At the age of 18, he married Anne Hathaway, with whom he had three children: Susanna and twins Hamnet and Judith. Sometime between 1585 and 1592, he began a successful career in London as an actor, writer, and part-owner of a playing company called the Lord Chamberlain's Men, later known as the King's Men. At age 49 (around 1613), he appears to have retired to Stratford, where he died three years later. (Source: Wikipedia)

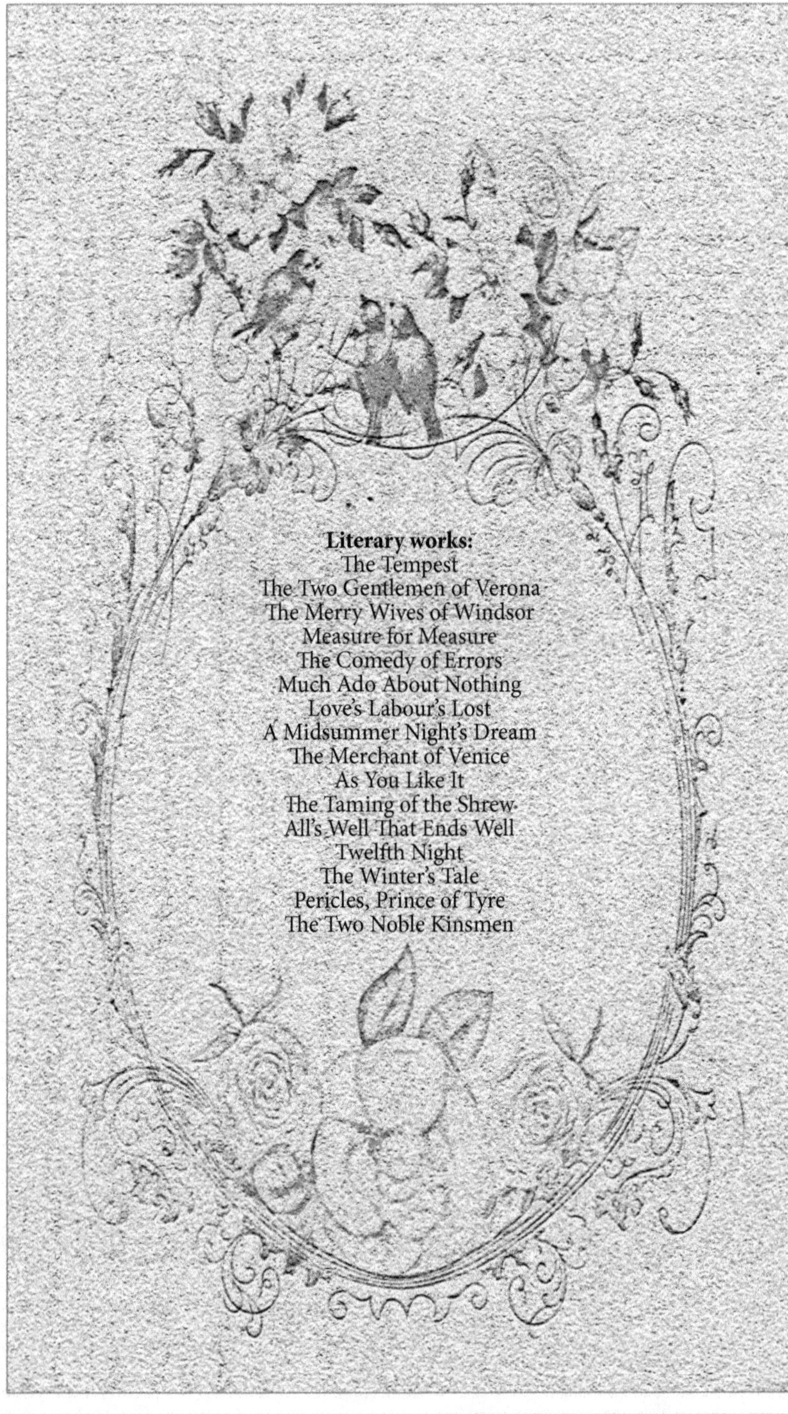

Literary works:
The Tempest
The Two Gentlemen of Verona
The Merry Wives of Windsor
Measure for Measure
The Comedy of Errors
Much Ado About Nothing
Love's Labour's Lost
A Midsummer Night's Dream
The Merchant of Venice
As You Like It
The Taming of the Shrew
All's Well That Ends Well
Twelfth Night
The Winter's Tale
Pericles, Prince of Tyre
The Two Noble Kinsmen

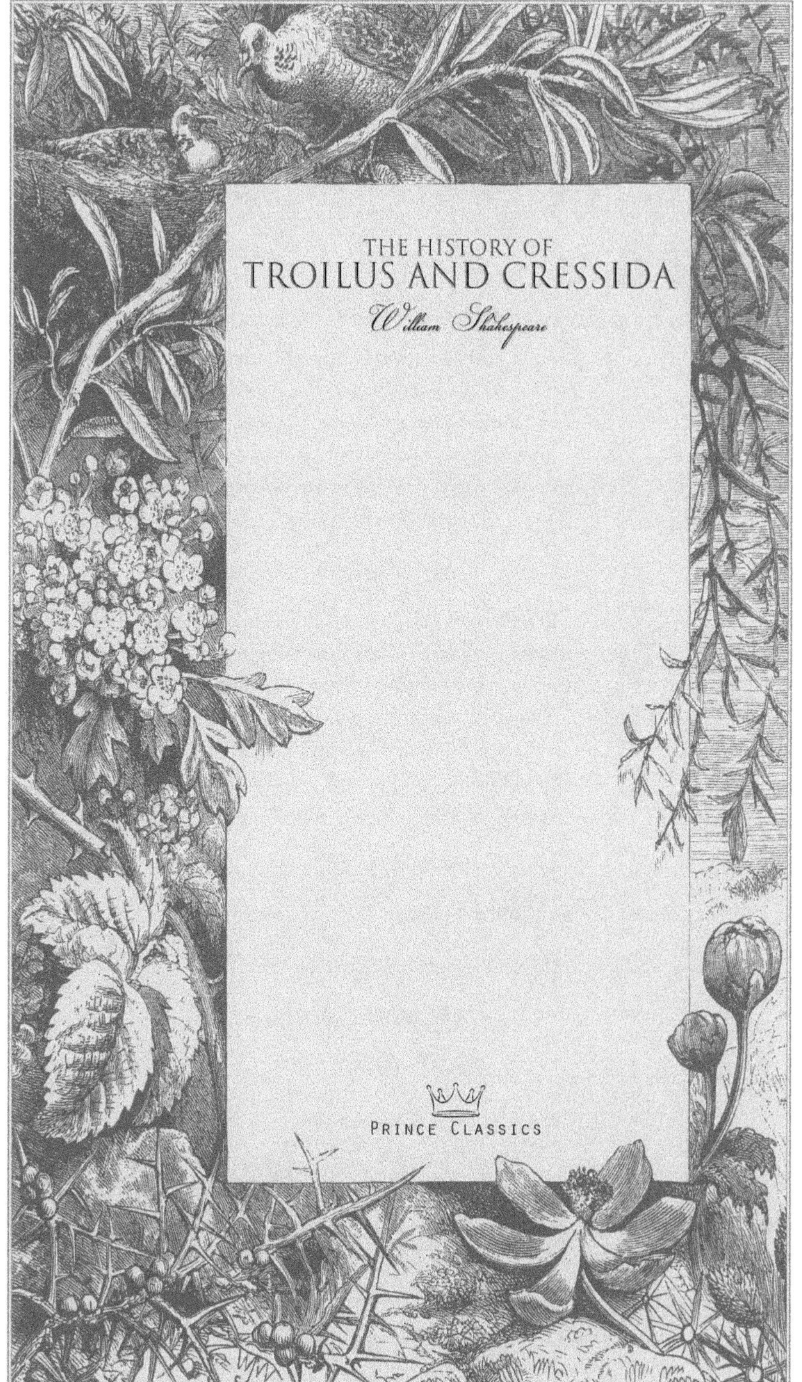

THE HISTORY OF
TROILUS AND CRESSIDA

William Shakespeare

PRINCE CLASSICS

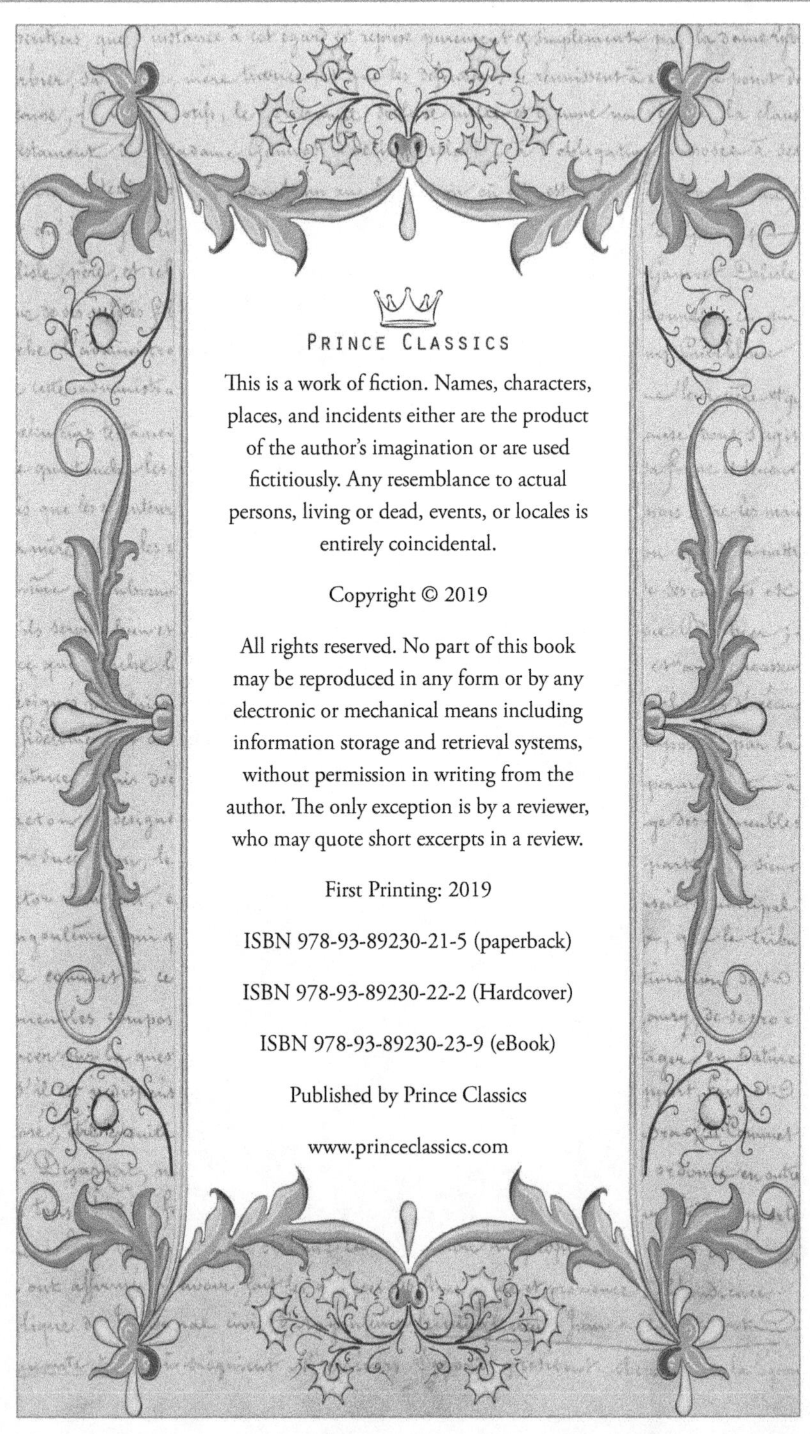

PRINCE CLASSICS

This is a work of fiction. Names, characters, places, and incidents either are the product of the author's imagination or are used fictitiously. Any resemblance to actual persons, living or dead, events, or locales is entirely coincidental.

First Printing: 2019

ISBN 978-93-89230-21-5 (paperback)

ISBN 978-93-89230-22-2 (Hardcover)

ISBN 978-93-89230-23-9 (eBook)

Published by Prince Classics

www.princeclassics.com

Contents

THE HISTORY OF
TROILUS AND CRESSIDA

Dramatis Personæ

PRIAM, King of Troy

His sons:

HECTOR

TROILUS

PARIS

DEIPHOBUS

HELENUS

MARGARELON, a bastard son of Priam

Trojan commanders:

AENEAS

ANTENOR

CALCHAS, a Trojan priest, taking part with the Greeks

PANDARUS, uncle to Cressida

AGAMEMNON, the Greek general

MENELAUS, his brother

Greek commanders:

ACHILLES

AJAX

ULYSSES

NESTOR

DIOMEDES

PATROCLUS

THERSITES, a deformed and scurrilous Greek

ALEXANDER, servant to Cressida

SERVANT to Troilus

SERVANT to Paris

SERVANT to Diomedes

HELEN, wife to Menelaus

ANDROMACHE, wife to Hector

CASSANDRA, daughter to Priam, a prophetess

CRESSIDA, daughter to Calchas

Trojan and Greek Soldiers, and Attendants

SCENE: Troy and the Greek camp before it

PROLOGUE

In Troy, there lies the scene. From isles of Greece
The princes orgulous, their high blood chaf'd,
Have to the port of Athens sent their ships
Fraught with the ministers and instruments
Of cruel war. Sixty and nine that wore
Their crownets regal from the Athenian bay
Put forth toward Phrygia; and their vow is made
To ransack Troy, within whose strong immures
The ravish'd Helen, Menelaus' queen,
With wanton Paris sleeps—and that's the quarrel.
To Tenedos they come,
And the deep-drawing barks do there disgorge
Their war-like fraughtage. Now on Dardan plains
The fresh and yet unbruised Greeks do pitch
Their brave pavilions: Priam's six-gated city,
Dardan, and Tymbria, Ilias, Chetas, Troien,
And Antenorides, with massy staples
And corresponsive and fulfilling bolts,
Stir up the sons of Troy.
Now expectation, tickling skittish spirits
On one and other side, Trojan and Greek,

Sets all on hazard. And hither am I come
A prologue arm'd, but not in confidence
Of author's pen or actor's voice, but suited
In like conditions as our argument,
To tell you, fair beholders, that our play
Leaps o'er the vaunt and firstlings of those broils,
Beginning in the middle; starting thence away,
To what may be digested in a play.
Like or find fault; do as your pleasures are;
Now good or bad, 'tis but the chance of war.

ACT I

SCENE I. Troy. Before PRIAM'S palace.

Enter Troilus armed, and Pandarus.

TROILUS.

Call here my varlet; I'll unarm again.

Why should I war without the walls of Troy

That find such cruel battle here within?

Each Trojan that is master of his heart,

Let him to field; Troilus, alas! hath none.

PANDARUS.

Will this gear ne'er be mended?

TROILUS.

The Greeks are strong, and skilful to their strength,

Fierce to their skill, and to their fierceness valiant;

But I am weaker than a woman's tear,

Tamer than sleep, fonder than ignorance,

Less valiant than the virgin in the night,

And skilless as unpractis'd infancy.

PANDARUS.

Well, I have told you enough of this; for my part, I'll not meddle nor make no farther. He that will have a cake out of the wheat must tarry the grinding.

TROILUS.

Have I not tarried?

PANDARUS.

Ay, the grinding; but you must tarry the bolting.

TROILUS.

Have I not tarried?

PANDARUS.

Ay, the bolting; but you must tarry the leavening.

TROILUS.

Still have I tarried.

PANDARUS.

Ay, to the leavening; but here's yet in the word 'hereafter' the kneading, the making of the cake, the heating of the oven, and the baking; nay, you must stay the cooling too, or you may chance burn your lips.

TROILUS.

Patience herself, what goddess e'er she be,

Doth lesser blench at suff'rance than I do.

At Priam's royal table do I sit;

And when fair Cressid comes into my thoughts,

So, traitor! 'when she comes'! when she is thence?

PANDARUS.

Well, she look'd yesternight fairer than ever I saw her look, or any woman else.

TROILUS.

I was about to tell thee: when my heart,

As wedged with a sigh, would rive in twain,

Lest Hector or my father should perceive me,

I have, as when the sun doth light a storm,

Buried this sigh in wrinkle of a smile.

But sorrow that is couch'd in seeming gladness

Is like that mirth fate turns to sudden sadness.

PANDARUS.

An her hair were not somewhat darker than Helen's, well, go to, there were no more comparison between the women. But, for my part, she is my kinswoman; I would not, as they term it, praise her, but I would somebody had heard her talk yesterday, as I did. I will not dispraise your sister Cassandra's wit; but—

TROILUS.

O Pandarus! I tell thee, Pandarus,

When I do tell thee there my hopes lie drown'd,

Reply not in how many fathoms deep

They lie indrench'd. I tell thee I am mad

In Cressid's love. Thou answer'st 'She is fair';

Pour'st in the open ulcer of my heart

Her eyes, her hair, her cheek, her gait, her voice,

Handlest in thy discourse. O! that her hand,

In whose comparison all whites are ink

Writing their own reproach; to whose soft seizure

The cygnet's down is harsh, and spirit of sense

Hard as the palm of ploughman! This thou tell'st me,

As true thou tell'st me, when I say I love her;

But, saying thus, instead of oil and balm,

Thou lay'st in every gash that love hath given me

The knife that made it.

PANDARUS.

I speak no more than truth.

TROILUS.

Thou dost not speak so much.

PANDARUS.

Faith, I'll not meddle in't. Let her be as she is: if she be fair, 'tis the better for her; and she be not, she has the mends in her own hands.

TROILUS.

Good Pandarus! How now, Pandarus!

PANDARUS.

I have had my labour for my travail, ill thought on of her and ill thought on of you; gone between and between, but small thanks for my labour.

TROILUS.

What! art thou angry, Pandarus? What! with me?

PANDARUS.

Because she's kin to me, therefore she's not so fair as Helen. And she were not kin to me, she would be as fair on Friday as Helen is on Sunday. But what care I? I care not and she were a blackamoor; 'tis all one to me.

TROILUS.

Say I she is not fair?

PANDARUS.

I do not care whether you do or no. She's a fool to stay behind her father. Let her to the Greeks; and so I'll tell her the next time I see her. For my part, I'll meddle nor make no more i' the matter.

TROILUS.

Pandarus—

PANDARUS.

Not I.

TROILUS.

Sweet Pandarus—

PANDARUS.

Pray you, speak no more to me: I will leave all as I found it, and there an end.

[Exit Pandarus. An alarum.]

TROILUS.

Peace, you ungracious clamours! Peace, rude sounds!

Fools on both sides! Helen must needs be fair,

When with your blood you daily paint her thus.

I cannot fight upon this argument;

It is too starv'd a subject for my sword.

But Pandarus, O gods! how do you plague me!

I cannot come to Cressid but by Pandar;

And he's as tetchy to be woo'd to woo

As she is stubborn-chaste against all suit.

Tell me, Apollo, for thy Daphne's love,

What Cressid is, what Pandar, and what we?

Her bed is India; there she lies, a pearl;

Between our Ilium and where she resides

Let it be call'd the wild and wandering flood;

Ourself the merchant, and this sailing Pandar

Our doubtful hope, our convoy, and our bark.

Alarum. Enter Aeneas.

AENEAS.

How now, Prince Troilus! Wherefore not afield?

TROILUS.

Because not there. This woman's answer sorts,

For womanish it is to be from thence.

What news, Aeneas, from the field today?

AENEAS.

That Paris is returned home, and hurt.

TROILUS.

By whom, Aeneas?

AENEAS.

Troilus, by Menelaus.

TROILUS.

Let Paris bleed: 'tis but a scar to scorn;

Paris is gor'd with Menelaus' horn.

[Alarum.]

AENEAS.

Hark what good sport is out of town today!

TROILUS.

Better at home, if 'would I might' were 'may.'

But to the sport abroad. Are you bound thither?

AENEAS.

In all swift haste.

TROILUS.

Come, go we then together.

[Exeunt.]

SCENE II. Troy. A street.

Enter Cressida and her man Alexander.

CRESSIDA.

Who were those went by?

ALEXANDER.

Queen Hecuba and Helen.

CRESSIDA.

And whither go they?

ALEXANDER.

Up to the eastern tower,

Whose height commands as subject all the vale,

To see the battle. Hector, whose patience

Is as a virtue fix'd, today was mov'd.

He chid Andromache, and struck his armourer;

And, like as there were husbandry in war,

Before the sun rose he was harness'd light,

And to the field goes he; where every flower

Did as a prophet weep what it foresaw

In Hector's wrath.

CRESSIDA.

What was his cause of anger?

ALEXANDER.

The noise goes, this: there is among the Greeks

A lord of Trojan blood, nephew to Hector;

They call him Ajax.

CRESSIDA.

Good; and what of him?

ALEXANDER.

They say he is a very man per se

And stands alone.

CRESSIDA.

So do all men, unless they are drunk, sick, or have no legs.

ALEXANDER.

This man, lady, hath robb'd many beasts of their particular additions: he is as valiant as the lion, churlish as the bear, slow as the elephant—a man into whom nature hath so crowded humours that his valour is crush'd into folly, his folly sauced with discretion. There is no man hath a virtue that he hath not a glimpse of, nor any man an attaint but he carries some stain of it; he is melancholy without cause and merry against the hair; he hath the joints of everything; but everything so out of joint that he is a gouty Briareus, many hands and no use, or purblind Argus, all eyes and no sight.

CRESSIDA.

But how should this man, that makes me smile, make Hector angry?

ALEXANDER.

They say he yesterday cop'd Hector in the battle and struck him down, the disdain and shame whereof hath ever since kept Hector fasting and waking.

Enter Pandarus.

CRESSIDA.

Who comes here?

ALEXANDER.

Madam, your uncle Pandarus.

CRESSIDA.

Hector's a gallant man.

ALEXANDER.

As may be in the world, lady.

PANDARUS.

What's that? What's that?

CRESSIDA.

Good morrow, uncle Pandarus.

PANDARUS.

Good morrow, cousin Cressid. What do you talk of?—Good morrow, Alexander.—How do you, cousin? When were you at Ilium?

CRESSIDA.

This morning, uncle.

PANDARUS.

What were you talking of when I came? Was Hector arm'd and gone ere you came to Ilium? Helen was not up, was she?

CRESSIDA.

Hector was gone; but Helen was not up.

PANDARUS.

E'en so. Hector was stirring early.

CRESSIDA.

That were we talking of, and of his anger.

PANDARUS.

Was he angry?

CRESSIDA.

So he says here.

PANDARUS.

True, he was so; I know the cause too; he'll lay about him today, I can tell them that. And there's Troilus will not come far behind him; let them take heed of Troilus, I can tell them that too.

CRESSIDA.

What, is he angry too?

PANDARUS.

Who, Troilus? Troilus is the better man of the two.

CRESSIDA.

O Jupiter! there's no comparison.

PANDARUS.

What, not between Troilus and Hector? Do you know a man if you see him?

CRESSIDA.

Ay, if I ever saw him before and knew him.

PANDARUS.

Well, I say Troilus is Troilus.

CRESSIDA.

Then you say as I say, for I am sure he is not Hector.

PANDARUS.

No, nor Hector is not Troilus in some degrees.

CRESSIDA.

'Tis just to each of them: he is himself.

PANDARUS.

Himself! Alas, poor Troilus! I would he were!

CRESSIDA.

So he is.

PANDARUS.

Condition I had gone barefoot to India.

CRESSIDA.

He is not Hector.

PANDARUS.

Himself! no, he's not himself. Would a' were himself! Well, the gods are above; time must friend or end. Well, Troilus, well! I would my heart were in her body! No, Hector is not a better man than Troilus.

CRESSIDA.

Excuse me.

PANDARUS.

He is elder.

CRESSIDA.

Pardon me, pardon me.

PANDARUS.

Th'other's not come to't; you shall tell me another tale when th'other's come to't. Hector shall not have his wit this year.

CRESSIDA.

He shall not need it if he have his own.

ANDARUS.

Nor his qualities.

CRESSIDA.

No matter.

PANDARUS.

Nor his beauty.

CRESSIDA.

'Twould not become him: his own's better.

PANDARUS.

You have no judgement, niece. Helen herself swore th'other day that Troilus, for a brown favour, for so 'tis, I must confess—not brown neither—

CRESSIDA.

No, but brown.

PANDARUS.

Faith, to say truth, brown and not brown.

CRESSIDA.

To say the truth, true and not true.

PANDARUS.

She prais'd his complexion above Paris.

CRESSIDA.

Why, Paris hath colour enough.

PANDARUS.

So he has.

CRESSIDA.

Then Troilus should have too much. If she prais'd him above, his complexion is higher than his; he having colour enough, and the other higher, is too flaming a praise for a good complexion. I had as lief Helen's golden tongue had commended Troilus for a copper nose.

PANDARUS.

I swear to you I think Helen loves him better than Paris.

CRESSIDA.

Then she's a merry Greek indeed.

PANDARUS.

Nay, I am sure she does. She came to him th'other day into the compass'd window—and you know he has not past three or four hairs on his chin—

CRESSIDA.

Indeed a tapster's arithmetic may soon bring his particulars therein to a total.

PANDARUS.

Why, he is very young, and yet will he within three pound lift as much as his brother Hector.

CRESSIDA.

Is he so young a man and so old a lifter?

PANDARUS.

But to prove to you that Helen loves him: she came and puts me her white hand to his cloven chin—

CRESSIDA.

Juno have mercy! How came it cloven?

PANDARUS.

Why, you know, 'tis dimpled. I think his smiling becomes him better than any man in all Phrygia.

CRESSIDA.

O, he smiles valiantly!

PANDARUS.

Does he not?

CRESSIDA.

O yes, an 'twere a cloud in autumn!

PANDARUS.

Why, go to, then! But to prove to you that Helen loves Troilus—

CRESSIDA.

Troilus will stand to the proof, if you'll prove it so.

PANDARUS.

Troilus! Why, he esteems her no more than I esteem an addle egg.

CRESSIDA.

If you love an addle egg as well as you love an idle head, you would eat chickens i' th' shell.

PANDARUS.

I cannot choose but laugh to think how she tickled his chin. Indeed, she has a marvell's white hand, I must needs confess.

CRESSIDA.

Without the rack.

PANDARUS.

And she takes upon her to spy a white hair on his chin.

CRESSIDA.

Alas, poor chin! Many a wart is richer.

PANDARUS.

But there was such laughing! Queen Hecuba laugh'd that her eyes ran o'er.

CRESSIDA.

With millstones.

PANDARUS.

And Cassandra laugh'd.

CRESSIDA.

But there was a more temperate fire under the pot of her eyes. Did her eyes run o'er too?

PANDARUS.

And Hector laugh'd.

CRESSIDA.

At what was all this laughing?

PANDARUS.

Marry, at the white hair that Helen spied on Troilus' chin.

CRESSIDA.

And't had been a green hair I should have laugh'd too.

PANDARUS.

They laugh'd not so much at the hair as at his pretty answer.

CRESSIDA.

What was his answer?

PANDARUS.

Quoth she 'Here's but two and fifty hairs on your chin, and one of them is white.'

CRESSIDA.

This is her question.

PANDARUS.

That's true; make no question of that. 'Two and fifty hairs,' quoth he 'and one white. That white hair is my father, and all the rest are his sons.' 'Jupiter!' quoth she 'which of these hairs is Paris my husband?' 'The forked one,' quoth he, 'pluck't out and give it him.' But there was such laughing! and Helen so blush'd, and Paris so chaf'd; and all the rest so laugh'd that it pass'd.

CRESSIDA.

So let it now; for it has been a great while going by.

PANDARUS.

Well, cousin, I told you a thing yesterday; think on't.

CRESSIDA.

So I do.

PANDARUS.

I'll be sworn 'tis true; he will weep you, and 'twere a man born in April.

CRESSIDA.

And I'll spring up in his tears, an 'twere a nettle against May.

[Sound a retreat.]

PANDARUS.

Hark! they are coming from the field. Shall we stand up here and see them as they pass toward Ilium? Good niece, do, sweet niece Cressida.

CRESSIDA.

At your pleasure.

PANDARUS.

Here, here, here's an excellent place; here we may see most bravely. I'll tell you them all by their names as they pass by; but mark Troilus above the rest.

[Aeneas passes.]

CRESSIDA.

Speak not so loud.

PANDARUS.

That's Aeneas. Is not that a brave man? He's one of the flowers of Troy, I can tell you. But mark Troilus; you shall see anon.

[Antenor passes.]

CRESSIDA.

Who's that?

PANDARUS.

That's Antenor. He has a shrewd wit, I can tell you; and he's a man good enough; he's one o' th' soundest judgements in Troy, whosoever, and a proper man of person. When comes Troilus? I'll show you Troilus anon. If he see me, you shall see him nod at me.

CRESSIDA.

Will he give you the nod?

PANDARUS.

You shall see.

CRESSIDA.

If he do, the rich shall have more.

[Hector passes.]

PANDARUS.

That's Hector, that, that, look you, that; there's a fellow! Go thy way, Hector! There's a brave man, niece. O brave Hector! Look how he looks. There's a countenance! Is't not a brave man?

CRESSIDA.

O, a brave man!

PANDARUS.

Is a' not? It does a man's heart good. Look you what hacks are on his helmet! Look you yonder, do you see? Look you there. There's no jesting; there's laying on; take't off who will, as they say. There be hacks.

CRESSIDA.

Be those with swords?

PANDARUS.

Swords! anything, he cares not; and the devil come to him, it's all one. By God's lid, it does one's heart good. Yonder comes Paris, yonder comes Paris.

[Paris passes.]

Look ye yonder, niece; is't not a gallant man too, is't not? Why, this is brave now. Who said he came hurt home today? He's not hurt. Why, this will do Helen's heart good now, ha! Would I could see Troilus now! You shall see Troilus anon.

[Helenus passes.]

CRESSIDA.

Who's that?

PANDARUS.

That's Helenus. I marvel where Troilus is. That's

Helenus. I think he went not forth today. That's Helenus.

CRESSIDA.

Can Helenus fight, uncle?

PANDARUS.

Helenus! no. Yes, he'll fight indifferent well. I marvel where Troilus is. Hark! do you not hear the people cry 'Troilus'?—Helenus is a priest.

CRESSIDA.

What sneaking fellow comes yonder?

[Troilus passes.]

PANDARUS.

Where? yonder? That's Deiphobus. 'Tis Troilus. There's a man, niece. Hem! Brave Troilus, the prince of chivalry!

CRESSIDA.

Peace, for shame, peace!

PANDARUS.

Mark him; note him. O brave Troilus! Look well upon him, niece; look you how his sword is bloodied, and his helm more hack'd than Hector's; and how he looks, and how he goes! O admirable youth! he never saw three and twenty. Go thy way, Troilus, go thy way. Had I a sister were a grace or a daughter a goddess, he should take his choice. O admirable man! Paris? Paris is dirt to him; and, I warrant, Helen, to change, would give an eye to boot.

CRESSIDA.

Here comes more.

[Common soldiers pass.]

PANDARUS.

Asses, fools, dolts! chaff and bran, chaff and bran! porridge after meat! I could live and die in the eyes of Troilus. Ne'er look, ne'er look; the eagles are gone. Crows and daws, crows and daws! I had rather be such a man as Troilus than Agamemnon and all Greece.

CRESSIDA.

There is amongst the Greeks Achilles, a better man than Troilus.

PANDARUS.

Achilles? A drayman, a porter, a very camel!

CRESSIDA.

Well, well.

PANDARUS.

Well, well! Why, have you any discretion? Have you any eyes? Do you know what a man is? Is not birth, beauty, good shape, discourse, manhood, learning, gentleness, virtue, youth, liberality, and such like, the spice and salt that season a man?

CRESSIDA.

Ay, a minc'd man; and then to be bak'd with no date in the pie, for then the man's date is out.

PANDARUS.

You are such a woman! A man knows not at what ward you lie.

CRESSIDA.

Upon my back, to defend my belly; upon my wit, to defend my wiles; upon my secrecy, to defend mine honesty; my mask, to defend my beauty;

and you, to defend all these; and at all these wards I lie, at a thousand watches.

PANDARUS.

Say one of your watches.

CRESSIDA.

Nay, I'll watch you for that; and that's one of the chiefest of them too. If I cannot ward what I would not have hit, I can watch you for telling how I took the blow; unless it swell past hiding, and then it's past watching.

PANDARUS.

You are such another!

Enter Troilus' Boy.

BOY.

Sir, my lord would instantly speak with you.

PANDARUS.

Where?

BOY.

At your own house; there he unarms him.

PANDARUS.

Good boy, tell him I come. [Exit Boy.] I doubt he be hurt. Fare ye well, good niece.

CRESSIDA.

Adieu, uncle.

PANDARUS.

I will be with you, niece, by and by.

CRESSIDA.

To bring, uncle.

PANDARUS.

Ay, a token from Troilus.

[Exit Pandarus.]

CRESSIDA.

By the same token, you are a bawd.

Words, vows, gifts, tears, and love's full sacrifice,

He offers in another's enterprise;

But more in Troilus thousand-fold I see

Than in the glass of Pandar's praise may be,

Yet hold I off. Women are angels, wooing:

Things won are done; joy's soul lies in the doing.

That she belov'd knows naught that knows not this:

Men prize the thing ungain'd more than it is.

That she was never yet that ever knew

Love got so sweet as when desire did sue;

Therefore this maxim out of love I teach:

'Achievement is command; ungain'd, beseech.'

Then though my heart's content firm love doth bear,

Nothing of that shall from mine eyes appear.

[Exit.]

SCENE III. The Grecian camp. Before AGAMEMNON'S tent.

Sennet. Enter Agamemnon, Nestor, Ulysses, Diomedes, Menelaus and others.

AGAMEMNON.

Princes,

What grief hath set these jaundies o'er your cheeks?

The ample proposition that hope makes

In all designs begun on earth below

Fails in the promis'd largeness; checks and disasters

Grow in the veins of actions highest rear'd,

As knots, by the conflux of meeting sap,

Infects the sound pine, and diverts his grain

Tortive and errant from his course of growth.

Nor, princes, is it matter new to us

That we come short of our suppose so far

That after seven years' siege yet Troy walls stand;

Sith every action that hath gone before,

Whereof we have record, trial did draw

Bias and thwart, not answering the aim,

And that unbodied figure of the thought

That gave't surmised shape. Why then, you princes,

Do you with cheeks abash'd behold our works

And call them shames, which are, indeed, naught else
But the protractive trials of great Jove
To find persistive constancy in men;
The fineness of which metal is not found
In fortune's love? For then the bold and coward,
The wise and fool, the artist and unread,
The hard and soft, seem all affin'd and kin.
But in the wind and tempest of her frown
Distinction, with a broad and powerful fan,
Puffing at all, winnows the light away;
And what hath mass or matter by itself
Lies rich in virtue and unmingled.

NESTOR.

With due observance of thy godlike seat,
Great Agamemnon, Nestor shall apply
Thy latest words. In the reproof of chance
Lies the true proof of men. The sea being smooth,
How many shallow bauble boats dare sail
Upon her patient breast, making their way
With those of nobler bulk!
But let the ruffian Boreas once enrage
The gentle Thetis, and anon behold
The strong-ribb'd bark through liquid mountains cut,

Bounding between the two moist elements

Like Perseus' horse. Where's then the saucy boat,

Whose weak untimber'd sides but even now

Co-rivall'd greatness? Either to harbour fled

Or made a toast for Neptune. Even so

Doth valour's show and valour's worth divide

In storms of fortune; for in her ray and brightness

The herd hath more annoyance by the breeze

Than by the tiger; but when the splitting wind

Makes flexible the knees of knotted oaks,

And flies fled under shade—why, then the thing of courage,

As rous'd with rage, with rage doth sympathise,

And with an accent tun'd in self-same key

Retorts to chiding fortune.

ULYSSES.

Agamemnon,

Thou great commander, nerve and bone of Greece,

Heart of our numbers, soul and only spirit

In whom the tempers and the minds of all

Should be shut up—hear what Ulysses speaks.

Besides th'applause and approbation

The which, [To Agamemnon] most mighty, for thy place and sway,

[To Nestor] And, thou most reverend, for thy stretch'd-out life,

I give to both your speeches—which were such
As Agamemnon and the hand of Greece
Should hold up high in brass; and such again
As venerable Nestor, hatch'd in silver,
Should with a bond of air, strong as the axle-tree
On which heaven rides, knit all the Greekish ears
To his experienc'd tongue—yet let it please both,
Thou great, and wise, to hear Ulysses speak.

AGAMEMNON.

Speak, Prince of Ithaca; and be't of less expect
That matter needless, of importless burden,
Divide thy lips than we are confident,
When rank Thersites opes his mastic jaws,
We shall hear music, wit, and oracle.

ULYSSES.

Troy, yet upon his basis, had been down,
And the great Hector's sword had lack'd a master,
But for these instances:
The specialty of rule hath been neglected;
And look how many Grecian tents do stand
Hollow upon this plain, so many hollow factions.
When that the general is not like the hive,
To whom the foragers shall all repair,

What honey is expected? Degree being vizarded,
Th'unworthiest shows as fairly in the mask.
The heavens themselves, the planets, and this centre,
Observe degree, priority, and place,
Insisture, course, proportion, season, form,
Office, and custom, in all line of order;
And therefore is the glorious planet Sol
In noble eminence enthron'd and spher'd
Amidst the other, whose med'cinable eye
Corrects the influence of evil planets,
And posts, like the commandment of a king,
Sans check, to good and bad. But when the planets
In evil mixture to disorder wander,
What plagues and what portents, what mutiny,
What raging of the sea, shaking of earth,
Commotion in the winds! Frights, changes, horrors,
Divert and crack, rend and deracinate,
The unity and married calm of states
Quite from their fixture! O, when degree is shak'd,
Which is the ladder of all high designs,
The enterprise is sick! How could communities,
Degrees in schools, and brotherhoods in cities,
Peaceful commerce from dividable shores,

The primogenity and due of birth,
Prerogative of age, crowns, sceptres, laurels,
But by degree stand in authentic place?
Take but degree away, untune that string,
And hark what discord follows! Each thing melts
In mere oppugnancy: the bounded waters
Should lift their bosoms higher than the shores,
And make a sop of all this solid globe;
Strength should be lord of imbecility,
And the rude son should strike his father dead;
Force should be right; or, rather, right and wrong—
Between whose endless jar justice resides—
Should lose their names, and so should justice too.
Then everything includes itself in power,
Power into will, will into appetite;
And appetite, an universal wolf,
So doubly seconded with will and power,
Must make perforce an universal prey,
And last eat up himself. Great Agamemnon,
This chaos, when degree is suffocate,
Follows the choking.
And this neglection of degree it is
That by a pace goes backward, with a purpose

It hath to climb. The general's disdain'd
By him one step below, he by the next,
That next by him beneath; so every step,
Exampl'd by the first pace that is sick
Of his superior, grows to an envious fever
Of pale and bloodless emulation.
And 'tis this fever that keeps Troy on foot,
Not her own sinews. To end a tale of length,
Troy in our weakness stands, not in her strength.

NESTOR.

Most wisely hath Ulysses here discover'd
The fever whereof all our power is sick.

AGAMEMNON.

The nature of the sickness found, Ulysses,
What is the remedy?

ULYSSES.

The great Achilles, whom opinion crowns
The sinew and the forehand of our host,
Having his ear full of his airy fame,
Grows dainty of his worth, and in his tent
Lies mocking our designs; with him Patroclus
Upon a lazy bed the livelong day
Breaks scurril jests;

And with ridiculous and awkward action—
Which, slanderer, he imitation calls—
He pageants us. Sometime, great Agamemnon,
Thy topless deputation he puts on;
And like a strutting player whose conceit
Lies in his hamstring, and doth think it rich
To hear the wooden dialogue and sound
'Twixt his stretch'd footing and the scaffoldage—
Such to-be-pitied and o'er-wrested seeming
He acts thy greatness in; and when he speaks
'Tis like a chime a-mending; with terms unsquar'd,
Which, from the tongue of roaring Typhon dropp'd,
Would seem hyperboles. At this fusty stuff
The large Achilles, on his press'd bed lolling,
From his deep chest laughs out a loud applause;
Cries 'Excellent! 'Tis Agamemnon right!
Now play me Nestor; hem, and stroke thy beard,
As he being drest to some oration.'
That's done—as near as the extremest ends
Of parallels, as like as Vulcan and his wife;
Yet god Achilles still cries 'Excellent!
'Tis Nestor right. Now play him me, Patroclus,
Arming to answer in a night alarm.'

And then, forsooth, the faint defects of age
Must be the scene of mirth: to cough and spit
And, with a palsy fumbling on his gorget,
Shake in and out the rivet. And at this sport
Sir Valour dies; cries 'O, enough, Patroclus;
Or give me ribs of steel! I shall split all
In pleasure of my spleen.' And in this fashion
All our abilities, gifts, natures, shapes,
Severals and generals of grace exact,
Achievements, plots, orders, preventions,
Excitements to the field or speech for truce,
Success or loss, what is or is not, serves
As stuff for these two to make paradoxes.

NESTOR.

And in the imitation of these twain—
Who, as Ulysses says, opinion crowns
With an imperial voice—many are infect.
Ajax is grown self-will'd and bears his head
In such a rein, in full as proud a place
As broad Achilles; keeps his tent like him;
Makes factious feasts; rails on our state of war
Bold as an oracle, and sets Thersites,
A slave whose gall coins slanders like a mint,

To match us in comparisons with dirt,
To weaken and discredit our exposure,
How rank soever rounded in with danger.

ULYSSES.

They tax our policy and call it cowardice,
Count wisdom as no member of the war,
Forestall prescience, and esteem no act
But that of hand. The still and mental parts
That do contrive how many hands shall strike
When fitness calls them on, and know, by measure
Of their observant toil, the enemies' weight—
Why, this hath not a finger's dignity:
They call this bed-work, mapp'ry, closet-war;
So that the ram that batters down the wall,
For the great swinge and rudeness of his poise,
They place before his hand that made the engine,
Or those that with the fineness of their souls
By reason guide his execution.

NESTOR.

Let this be granted, and Achilles' horse
Makes many Thetis' sons.

[Tucket.]

AGAMEMNON.

What trumpet? Look, Menelaus.

MENELAUS.

From Troy.

Enter Aeneas.

AGAMEMNON.

What would you fore our tent?

AENEAS.

Is this great Agamemnon's tent, I pray you?

AGAMEMNON.

Even this.

AENEAS.

May one that is a herald and a prince

Do a fair message to his kingly eyes?

AGAMEMNON.

With surety stronger than Achilles' arm

Fore all the Greekish heads, which with one voice

Call Agamemnon head and general.

AENEAS.

Fair leave and large security. How may

A stranger to those most imperial looks

Know them from eyes of other mortals?

AGAMEMNON.

How?

AENEAS.

Ay;

I ask, that I might waken reverence,

And bid the cheek be ready with a blush

Modest as morning when she coldly eyes

The youthful Phoebus.

Which is that god in office, guiding men?

Which is the high and mighty Agamemnon?

AGAMEMNON.

This Trojan scorns us, or the men of Troy

Are ceremonious courtiers.

AENEAS.

Courtiers as free, as debonair, unarm'd,

As bending angels; that's their fame in peace.

But when they would seem soldiers, they have galls,

Good arms, strong joints, true swords; and, Jove's accord,

Nothing so full of heart. But peace, Aeneas,

Peace, Trojan; lay thy finger on thy lips.

The worthiness of praise distains his worth,

If that the prais'd himself bring the praise forth;

But what the repining enemy commends,

That breath fame blows; that praise, sole pure, transcends.

AGAMEMNON.

Sir, you of Troy, call you yourself Aeneas?

AENEAS.

Ay, Greek, that is my name.

AGAMEMNON.

What's your affairs, I pray you?

AENEAS.

Sir, pardon; 'tis for Agamemnon's ears.

AGAMEMNON

He hears naught privately that comes from Troy.

AENEAS.

Nor I from Troy come not to whisper with him;
I bring a trumpet to awake his ear,
To set his sense on the attentive bent,
And then to speak.

AGAMEMNON.

Speak frankly as the wind;
It is not Agamemnon's sleeping hour.
That thou shalt know, Trojan, he is awake,
He tells thee so himself.

AENEAS.

Trumpet, blow loud,
Send thy brass voice through all these lazy tents;
And every Greek of mettle, let him know
What Troy means fairly shall be spoke aloud.

[Sound trumpet.]

We have, great Agamemnon, here in Troy

A prince called Hector—Priam is his father—
Who in this dull and long-continued truce
Is resty grown; he bade me take a trumpet
And to this purpose speak: Kings, princes, lords!
If there be one among the fair'st of Greece
That holds his honour higher than his ease,
That feeds his praise more than he fears his peril,
That knows his valour and knows not his fear,
That loves his mistress more than in confession
With truant vows to her own lips he loves,
And dare avow her beauty and her worth
In other arms than hers—to him this challenge.
Hector, in view of Trojans and of Greeks,
Shall make it good or do his best to do it:
He hath a lady wiser, fairer, truer,
Than ever Greek did couple in his arms;
And will tomorrow with his trumpet call
Mid-way between your tents and walls of Troy
To rouse a Grecian that is true in love.
If any come, Hector shall honour him;
If none, he'll say in Troy, when he retires,
The Grecian dames are sunburnt and not worth
The splinter of a lance. Even so much.

AGAMEMNON.

This shall be told our lovers, Lord Aeneas.
If none of them have soul in such a kind,
We left them all at home. But we are soldiers;
And may that soldier a mere recreant prove
That means not, hath not, or is not in love.
If then one is, or hath, or means to be,
That one meets Hector; if none else, I am he.

NESTOR.

Tell him of Nestor, one that was a man
When Hector's grandsire suck'd. He is old now;
But if there be not in our Grecian host
A noble man that hath one spark of fire
To answer for his love, tell him from me
I'll hide my silver beard in a gold beaver,
And in my vambrace put this wither'd brawns,
And meeting him, will tell him that my lady
Was fairer than his grandam, and as chaste
As may be in the world. His youth in flood,
I'll prove this troth with my three drops of blood.

AENEAS.

Now heavens forfend such scarcity of youth!

ULYSSES.

Amen.

AGAMEMNON.

Fair Lord Aeneas, let me touch your hand;

To our pavilion shall I lead you, sir.

Achilles shall have word of this intent;

So shall each lord of Greece, from tent to tent.

Yourself shall feast with us before you go,

And find the welcome of a noble foe.

[Exeunt all but Ulysses and Nestor.]

ULYSSES.

Nestor!

NESTOR.

What says Ulysses?

ULYSSES.

I have a young conception in my brain;

Be you my time to bring it to some shape.

NESTOR.

What is't?

ULYSSES.

This 'tis:

Blunt wedges rive hard knots. The seeded pride

That hath to this maturity blown up

In rank Achilles must or now be cropp'd

Or, shedding, breed a nursery of like evil

To overbulk us all.

NESTOR.

Well, and how?

ULYSSES.

This challenge that the gallant Hector sends,

However it is spread in general name,

Relates in purpose only to Achilles.

NESTOR.

True. The purpose is perspicuous even as substance

Whose grossness little characters sum up;

And, in the publication, make no strain

But that Achilles, were his brain as barren

As banks of Libya—though, Apollo knows,

'Tis dry enough—will with great speed of judgement,

Ay, with celerity, find Hector's purpose

Pointing on him.

ULYSSES.

And wake him to the answer, think you?

NESTOR.

Why, 'tis most meet. Who may you else oppose

That can from Hector bring those honours off,

If not Achilles? Though 't be a sportful combat,

Yet in this trial much opinion dwells

For here the Trojans taste our dear'st repute
With their fin'st palate; and trust to me, Ulysses,
Our imputation shall be oddly pois'd
In this vile action; for the success,
Although particular, shall give a scantling
Of good or bad unto the general;
And in such indexes, although small pricks
To their subsequent volumes, there is seen
The baby figure of the giant mass
Of things to come at large. It is suppos'd
He that meets Hector issues from our choice;
And choice, being mutual act of all our souls,
Makes merit her election, and doth boil,
As 'twere from forth us all, a man distill'd
Out of our virtues; who miscarrying,
What heart receives from hence a conquering part,
To steel a strong opinion to themselves?
Which entertain'd, limbs are his instruments,
In no less working than are swords and bows
Directive by the limbs.

ULYSSES.

Give pardon to my speech. Therefore 'tis meet
Achilles meet not Hector. Let us, like merchants,

First show foul wares, and think perchance they'll sell;
If not, the lustre of the better shall exceed
By showing the worse first. Do not consent
That ever Hector and Achilles meet;
For both our honour and our shame in this
Are dogg'd with two strange followers.

NESTOR.

I see them not with my old eyes. What are they?

ULYSSES.

What glory our Achilles shares from Hector,
Were he not proud, we all should share with him;
But he already is too insolent;
And it were better parch in Afric sun
Than in the pride and salt scorn of his eyes,
Should he scape Hector fair. If he were foil'd,
Why, then we do our main opinion crush
In taint of our best man. No, make a lott'ry;
And, by device, let blockish Ajax draw
The sort to fight with Hector. Among ourselves
Give him allowance for the better man;
For that will physic the great Myrmidon,
Who broils in loud applause, and make him fall
His crest, that prouder than blue Iris bends.

If the dull brainless Ajax come safe off,
We'll dress him up in voices; if he fail,
Yet go we under our opinion still
That we have better men. But, hit or miss,
Our project's life this shape of sense assumes—
Ajax employ'd plucks down Achilles' plumes.

NESTOR.

Now, Ulysses, I begin to relish thy advice;
And I will give a taste thereof forthwith
To Agamemnon. Go we to him straight.
Two curs shall tame each other: pride alone
Must tarre the mastiffs on, as 'twere their bone.

[Exeunt.]

ACT II

SCENE I. The Grecian camp.

Enter Ajax and Thersites.

AJAX.

Thersites!

THERSITES.

Agamemnon—how if he had boils, full, all over, generally?

AJAX.

Thersites!

THERSITES.

And those boils did run—say so. Did not the general run then? Were not that a botchy core?

AJAX.

Dog!

THERSITES.

Then there would come some matter from him;

I see none now.

AJAX.

Thou bitch-wolf's son, canst thou not hear? Feel, then.

[Strikes him.]

THERSITES.

The plague of Greece upon thee, thou mongrel beef-witted lord!

AJAX.

Speak, then, thou unsalted leaven, speak. I will beat thee into handsomeness.

THERSITES.

I shall sooner rail thee into wit and holiness; but I think thy horse will sooner con an oration than thou learn a prayer without book. Thou canst strike, canst thou? A red murrain o' thy jade's tricks!

AJAX.

Toadstool, learn me the proclamation.

THERSITES.

Dost thou think I have no sense, thou strikest me thus?

AJAX.

The proclamation!

THERSITES.

Thou art proclaim'd fool, I think.

AJAX.

Do not, porpentine, do not; my fingers itch.

THERSITES.

I would thou didst itch from head to foot and I had the scratching of thee; I would make thee the loathsomest scab in Greece. When thou art forth in the incursions, thou strikest as slow as another.

AJAX.

I say, the proclamation.

THERSITES.

Thou grumblest and railest every hour on Achilles; and thou art as full of envy at his greatness as Cerberus is at Proserpina's beauty—ay, that thou bark'st at him.

AJAX.

Mistress Thersites!

THERSITES.

Thou shouldst strike him.

AJAX.

Cobloaf!

THERSITES.

He would pun thee into shivers with his fist, as a sailor breaks a biscuit.

AJAX.

You whoreson cur!

[Strikes him.]

THERSITES.

Do, do.

AJAX.

Thou stool for a witch!

THERSITES.

Ay, do, do; thou sodden-witted lord! Thou hast no more brain than I have in mine elbows; an asinico may tutor thee. You scurvy valiant ass! Thou art here but to thrash Trojans, and thou art bought and sold among those of any wit like a barbarian slave. If thou use to beat me, I will begin at thy heel and tell what thou art by inches, thou thing of no bowels, thou!

AJAX.

You dog!

THERSITES.

You scurvy lord!

AJAX.

You cur!

[Strikes him.]

THERSITES.

Mars his idiot! Do, rudeness; do, camel; do, do.

Enter Achilles and Patroclus.

ACHILLES.

Why, how now, Ajax! Wherefore do ye thus?

How now, Thersites! What's the matter, man?

THERSITES.

You see him there, do you?

ACHILLES.

Ay; what's the matter?

THERSITES.

Nay, look upon him.

ACHILLES.

So I do. What's the matter?

THERSITES.

Nay, but regard him well.

ACHILLES.

Well! why, so I do.

THERSITES.

But yet you look not well upon him; for whosomever you take him to be, he is Ajax.

ACHILLES.

I know that, fool.

THERSITES.

Ay, but that fool knows not himself.

AJAX.

Therefore I beat thee.

THERSITES.

Lo, lo, lo, lo, what modicums of wit he utters! His evasions have ears thus long. I have bobb'd his brain more than he has beat my bones. I will buy nine sparrows for a penny, and his pia mater is not worth the ninth part of a sparrow. This lord, Achilles—Ajax, who wears his wit in his belly and his guts in his head—I'll tell you what I say of him.

ACHILLES.

What?

THERSITES.

I say this Ajax—

[Ajax offers to strike him.]

ACHILLES.

Nay, good Ajax.

THERSITES.

Has not so much wit—

ACHILLES.

Nay, I must hold you.

THERSITES.

As will stop the eye of Helen's needle, for whom he comes to fight.

ACHILLES.

Peace, fool.

THERSITES.

I would have peace and quietness, but the fool will not— he there; that he; look you there.

AJAX.

O thou damned cur! I shall—

ACHILLES.

Will you set your wit to a fool's?

THERSITES.

No, I warrant you, the fool's will shame it.

PATROCLUS.

Good words, Thersites.

ACHILLES.

What's the quarrel?

AJAX.

I bade the vile owl go learn me the tenour of the proclamation, and he rails upon me.

THERSITES.

I serve thee not.

AJAX.

Well, go to, go to.

THERSITES.

I serve here voluntary.

ACHILLES.

Your last service was suff'rance; 'twas not voluntary. No man is beaten voluntary. Ajax was here the voluntary, and you as under an impress.

THERSITES.

E'en so; a great deal of your wit too lies in your sinews, or else there be liars. Hector shall have a great catch and knock out either of your brains: a' were as good crack a fusty nut with no kernel.

ACHILLES.

What, with me too, Thersites?

THERSITES.

There's Ulysses and old Nestor—whose wit was mouldy ere your grandsires had nails on their toes—yoke you like draught oxen, and make you plough up the wars.

ACHILLES.

What, what?

THERSITES.

Yes, good sooth. To Achilles, to Ajax, to—

AJAX.

I shall cut out your tongue.

THERSITES.

'Tis no matter; I shall speak as much as thou afterwards.

PATROCLUS.

No more words, Thersites; peace!

THERSITES.

I will hold my peace when Achilles' brach bids me, shall I?

ACHILLES.

There's for you, Patroclus.

THERSITES.

I will see you hang'd like clotpoles ere I come any more to your tents. I will keep where there is wit stirring, and leave the faction of fools.

[Exit.]

PATROCLUS.

A good riddance.

ACHILLES.

Marry, this, sir, is proclaim'd through all our host,

That Hector, by the fifth hour of the sun,

Will with a trumpet 'twixt our tents and Troy,

Tomorrow morning, call some knight to arms

That hath a stomach; and such a one that dare

Maintain I know not what; 'tis trash. Farewell.

AJAX.

Farewell. Who shall answer him?

ACHILLES.

I know not; 'tis put to lott'ry, otherwise,

He knew his man.

AJAX.

O, meaning you? I will go learn more of it.

[Exeunt.]

SCENE II. Troy. PRIAM'S palace.

Enter Priam, Hector, Troilus, Paris and Helenus.

PRIAM.

After so many hours, lives, speeches spent,

Thus once again says Nestor from the Greeks:

'Deliver Helen, and all damage else—

As honour, loss of time, travail, expense,

Wounds, friends, and what else dear that is consum'd

In hot digestion of this cormorant war—

Shall be struck off.' Hector, what say you to't?

HECTOR.

Though no man lesser fears the Greeks than I,

As far as toucheth my particular,

Yet, dread Priam,

There is no lady of more softer bowels,

More spongy to suck in the sense of fear,

More ready to cry out 'Who knows what follows?'

Than Hector is. The wound of peace is surety,

Surety secure; but modest doubt is call'd

The beacon of the wise, the tent that searches

To th' bottom of the worst. Let Helen go.

Since the first sword was drawn about this question,

Every tithe soul 'mongst many thousand dismes
Hath been as dear as Helen—I mean, of ours.
If we have lost so many tenths of ours
To guard a thing not ours, nor worth to us,
Had it our name, the value of one ten,
What merit's in that reason which denies
The yielding of her up?

TROILUS.

Fie, fie, my brother!
Weigh you the worth and honour of a king,
So great as our dread father's, in a scale
Of common ounces? Will you with counters sum
The past-proportion of his infinite,
And buckle in a waist most fathomless
With spans and inches so diminutive
As fears and reasons? Fie, for godly shame!

HELENUS.

No marvel though you bite so sharp of reasons,
You are so empty of them. Should not our father
Bear the great sway of his affairs with reason,
Because your speech hath none that tells him so?

TROILUS.

You are for dreams and slumbers, brother priest;

You fur your gloves with reason. Here are your reasons:

You know an enemy intends you harm;

You know a sword employ'd is perilous,

And reason flies the object of all harm.

Who marvels, then, when Helenus beholds

A Grecian and his sword, if he do set

The very wings of reason to his heels

And fly like chidden Mercury from Jove,

Or like a star disorb'd? Nay, if we talk of reason,

Let's shut our gates and sleep. Manhood and honour

Should have hare hearts, would they but fat their thoughts

With this cramm'd reason. Reason and respect

Make livers pale and lustihood deject.

HECTOR.

Brother, she is not worth what she doth cost the keeping.

TROILUS.

What's aught but as 'tis valued?

HECTOR.

But value dwells not in particular will:

It holds his estimate and dignity

As well wherein 'tis precious of itself

As in the prizer. 'Tis mad idolatry

To make the service greater than the god,

And the will dotes that is attributive
To what infectiously itself affects,
Without some image of th'affected merit.

TROILUS.

I take today a wife, and my election
Is led on in the conduct of my will;
My will enkindled by mine eyes and ears,
Two traded pilots 'twixt the dangerous shores
Of will and judgement: how may I avoid,
Although my will distaste what it elected,
The wife I chose? There can be no evasion
To blench from this and to stand firm by honour.
We turn not back the silks upon the merchant
When we have soil'd them; nor the remainder viands
We do not throw in unrespective sieve,
Because we now are full. It was thought meet
Paris should do some vengeance on the Greeks;
Your breath with full consent bellied his sails;
The seas and winds, old wranglers, took a truce,
And did him service. He touch'd the ports desir'd;
And for an old aunt whom the Greeks held captive
He brought a Grecian queen, whose youth and freshness
Wrinkles Apollo's, and makes stale the morning.

Why keep we her? The Grecians keep our aunt.
Is she worth keeping? Why, she is a pearl
Whose price hath launch'd above a thousand ships,
And turn'd crown'd kings to merchants.
If you'll avouch 'twas wisdom Paris went—
As you must needs, for you all cried 'Go, go'—
If you'll confess he brought home worthy prize—
As you must needs, for you all clapp'd your hands,
And cried 'Inestimable!'—why do you now
The issue of your proper wisdoms rate,
And do a deed that never Fortune did—
Beggar the estimation which you priz'd
Richer than sea and land? O theft most base,
That we have stol'n what we do fear to keep!
But thieves unworthy of a thing so stol'n
That in their country did them that disgrace
We fear to warrant in our native place!

CASSANDRA.

[Within.] Cry, Trojans, cry.

PRIAM.

What noise, what shriek is this?

TROILUS.

'Tis our mad sister; I do know her voice.

CASSANDRA.

[Within.] Cry, Trojans.

HECTOR.

It is Cassandra.

Enter Cassandra, raving.

CASSANDRA.

Cry, Trojans, cry. Lend me ten thousand eyes,
And I will fill them with prophetic tears.

HECTOR.

Peace, sister, peace.

CASSANDRA.

Virgins and boys, mid-age and wrinkled eld,
Soft infancy, that nothing canst but cry,
Add to my clamours. Let us pay betimes
A moiety of that mass of moan to come.
Cry, Trojans, cry. Practise your eyes with tears.
Troy must not be, nor goodly Ilion stand;
Our firebrand brother, Paris, burns us all.
Cry, Trojans, cry, A Helen and a woe!
Cry, cry. Troy burns, or else let Helen go.

[Exit.]

HECTOR.

Now, youthful Troilus, do not these high strains
Of divination in our sister work

Some touches of remorse? Or is your blood
So madly hot, that no discourse of reason,
Nor fear of bad success in a bad cause,
Can qualify the same?

TROILUS.

Why, brother Hector,
We may not think the justness of each act
Such and no other than event doth form it;
Nor once deject the courage of our minds
Because Cassandra's mad. Her brain-sick raptures
Cannot distaste the goodness of a quarrel
Which hath our several honours all engag'd
To make it gracious. For my private part,
I am no more touch'd than all Priam's sons;
And Jove forbid there should be done amongst us
Such things as might offend the weakest spleen
To fight for and maintain.

PARIS.

Else might the world convince of levity
As well my undertakings as your counsels;
But I attest the gods, your full consent
Gave wings to my propension, and cut off
All fears attending on so dire a project.

For what, alas, can these my single arms?
What propugnation is in one man's valour
To stand the push and enmity of those
This quarrel would excite? Yet I protest,
Were I alone to pass the difficulties,
And had as ample power as I have will,
Paris should ne'er retract what he hath done,
Nor faint in the pursuit.

PRIAM.

Paris, you speak
Like one besotted on your sweet delights.
You have the honey still, but these the gall;
So to be valiant is no praise at all.

PARIS.

Sir, I propose not merely to myself
The pleasures such a beauty brings with it;
But I would have the soil of her fair rape
Wip'd off in honourable keeping her.
What treason were it to the ransack'd queen,
Disgrace to your great worths, and shame to me,
Now to deliver her possession up
On terms of base compulsion! Can it be,
That so degenerate a strain as this

Should once set footing in your generous bosoms?
There's not the meanest spirit on our party
Without a heart to dare or sword to draw
When Helen is defended; nor none so noble
Whose life were ill bestow'd or death unfam'd,
Where Helen is the subject. Then, I say,
Well may we fight for her whom we know well
The world's large spaces cannot parallel.

HECTOR.

Paris and Troilus, you have both said well;
And on the cause and question now in hand
Have gloz'd, but superficially; not much
Unlike young men, whom Aristotle thought
Unfit to hear moral philosophy.
The reasons you allege do more conduce
To the hot passion of distemp'red blood
Than to make up a free determination
'Twixt right and wrong; for pleasure and revenge
Have ears more deaf than adders to the voice
Of any true decision. Nature craves
All dues be rend'red to their owners. Now,
What nearer debt in all humanity
Than wife is to the husband? If this law

Of nature be corrupted through affection;
And that great minds, of partial indulgence
To their benumbed wills, resist the same;
There is a law in each well-order'd nation
To curb those raging appetites that are
Most disobedient and refractory.
If Helen, then, be wife to Sparta's king—
As it is known she is—these moral laws
Of nature and of nations speak aloud
To have her back return'd. Thus to persist
In doing wrong extenuates not wrong,
But makes it much more heavy. Hector's opinion
Is this, in way of truth. Yet, ne'ertheless,
My spritely brethren, I propend to you
In resolution to keep Helen still;
For 'tis a cause that hath no mean dependence
Upon our joint and several dignities.

TROILUS.

Why, there you touch'd the life of our design.
Were it not glory that we more affected
Than the performance of our heaving spleens,
I would not wish a drop of Trojan blood
Spent more in her defence. But, worthy Hector,

She is a theme of honour and renown,
A spur to valiant and magnanimous deeds,
Whose present courage may beat down our foes,
And fame in time to come canonize us;
For I presume brave Hector would not lose
So rich advantage of a promis'd glory
As smiles upon the forehead of this action
For the wide world's revenue.

HECTOR.

I am yours,
You valiant offspring of great Priamus.
I have a roisting challenge sent amongst
The dull and factious nobles of the Greeks
Will strike amazement to their drowsy spirits.
I was advertis'd their great general slept,
Whilst emulation in the army crept.
This, I presume, will wake him.

[Exeunt.]

SCENE III. The Grecian camp. Before the tent of ACHILLES.

Enter Thersites, solus.

THERSITES.

How now, Thersites! What, lost in the labyrinth of thy fury? Shall the elephant Ajax carry it thus? He beats me, and I rail at him. O worthy satisfaction! Would it were otherwise: that I could beat him, whilst he rail'd at me! 'Sfoot, I'll learn to conjure and raise devils, but I'll see some issue of my spiteful execrations. Then there's Achilles, a rare engineer! If Troy be not taken till these two undermine it, the walls will stand till they fall of themselves. O thou great thunder-darter of Olympus, forget that thou art Jove, the king of gods, and, Mercury, lose all the serpentine craft of thy caduceus, if ye take not that little little less than little wit from them that they have! which short-arm'd ignorance itself knows is so abundant scarce, it will not in circumvention deliver a fly from a spider without drawing their massy irons and cutting the web. After this, the vengeance on the whole camp! or, rather, the Neapolitan bone-ache! for that, methinks, is the curse depending on those that war for a placket. I have said my prayers; and devil Envy say 'Amen.' What ho! my Lord Achilles!

Enter Patroclus.

PATROCLUS.

Who's there? Thersites! Good Thersites, come in and rail.

THERSITES.

If I could a' rememb'red a gilt counterfeit, thou wouldst not have slipp'd out of my contemplation; but it is no matter; thyself upon thyself! The common curse of mankind, folly and ignorance, be thine in great revenue! Heaven bless thee from a tutor, and discipline come not near thee! Let thy blood be thy direction till thy death. Then if she that lays thee out says thou art a fair corse, I'll be sworn and sworn upon't she never shrouded any but lazars. Amen. Where's Achilles?

PATROCLUS.

What, art thou devout? Wast thou in prayer?

THERSITES.

Ay, the heavens hear me!

PATROCLUS.

Amen.

Enter Achilles.

ACHILLES.

Who's there?

PATROCLUS.

Thersites, my lord.

ACHILLES.

Where, where? O, where? Art thou come? Why, my cheese, my digestion, why hast thou not served thyself in to my table so many meals? Come, what's Agamemnon?

THERSITES.

Thy commander, Achilles. Then tell me, Patroclus, what's Achilles?

PATROCLUS.

Thy lord, Thersites. Then tell me, I pray thee, what's Thersites?

THERSITES.

Thy knower, Patroclus. Then tell me, Patroclus, what art thou?

PATROCLUS.

Thou must tell that knowest.

ACHILLES.

O, tell, tell,

THERSITES.

I'll decline the whole question. Agamemnon commands Achilles; Achilles is my lord; I am Patroclus' knower; and Patroclus is a fool.

PATROCLUS.

You rascal!

THERSITES.

Peace, fool! I have not done.

ACHILLES.

He is a privileg'd man. Proceed, Thersites.

THERSITES.

Agamemnon is a fool; Achilles is a fool; Thersites is a fool; and, as aforesaid, Patroclus is a fool.

ACHILLES.

Derive this; come.

THERSITES.

Agamemnon is a fool to offer to command Achilles; Achilles is a fool to be commanded of Agamemnon; Thersites is a fool to serve such a fool; and this Patroclus is a fool positive.

PATROCLUS.

Why am I a fool?

THERSITES.

Make that demand of the Creator. It suffices me thou art. Look you, who comes here?

Enter Agamemnon, Ulysses, Nestor, Diomedes, Ajax and Calchas.

ACHILLES.

Come, Patroclus, I'll speak with nobody. Come in with me, Thersites.

[Exit.]

THERSITES.

Here is such patchery, such juggling, and such knavery. All the argument is a whore and a cuckold—a good quarrel to draw emulous factions and bleed to death upon. Now the dry serpigo on the subject, and war and lechery confound all!

[Exit.]

AGAMEMNON.

Where is Achilles?

PATROCLUS.

Within his tent; but ill-dispos'd, my lord.

AGAMEMNON.

Let it be known to him that we are here.

He sate our messengers; and we lay by

Our appertainings, visiting of him.

Let him be told so; lest, perchance, he think

We dare not move the question of our place

Or know not what we are.

PATROCLUS.

I shall say so to him.

[Exit.]

ULYSSES.

We saw him at the opening of his tent.

He is not sick.

AJAX.

Yes, lion-sick, sick of proud heart. You may call it melancholy, if you will favour the man; but, by my head, 'tis pride. But why, why? Let him show us a cause. A word, my lord.

[Takes Agamemnon aside.]

NESTOR.

What moves Ajax thus to bay at him?

ULYSSES.

Achilles hath inveigled his fool from him.

NESTOR.

Who, Thersites?

ULYSSES.

He.

NESTOR.

Then will Ajax lack matter, if he have lost his argument.

ULYSSES.

No; you see he is his argument that has his argument, Achilles.

NESTOR.

All the better; their fraction is more our wish than their faction. But it was a strong composure a fool could disunite!

ULYSSES.

The amity that wisdom knits not, folly may easily untie.

Re-enter Patroclus.

Here comes Patroclus.

NESTOR.

No Achilles with him.

ULYSSES.

The elephant hath joints, but none for courtesy; his legs are legs for necessity, not for flexure.

PATROCLUS.

Achilles bids me say he is much sorry

If any thing more than your sport and pleasure

Did move your greatness and this noble state

To call upon him; he hopes it is no other

But for your health and your digestion sake,

An after-dinner's breath.

AGAMEMNON.

Hear you, Patroclus.

We are too well acquainted with these answers;

But his evasion, wing'd thus swift with scorn,

Cannot outfly our apprehensions.

Much attribute he hath, and much the reason

Why we ascribe it to him. Yet all his virtues,

Not virtuously on his own part beheld,

Do in our eyes begin to lose their gloss;

Yea, like fair fruit in an unwholesome dish,

Are like to rot untasted. Go and tell him

We come to speak with him; and you shall not sin

If you do say we think him over-proud
And under-honest, in self-assumption greater
Than in the note of judgement; and worthier than himself
Here tend the savage strangeness he puts on,
Disguise the holy strength of their command,
And underwrite in an observing kind
His humorous predominance; yea, watch
His course and time, his ebbs and flows, as if
The passage and whole stream of this commencement
Rode on his tide. Go tell him this, and add
That if he overhold his price so much
We'll none of him, but let him, like an engine
Not portable, lie under this report:
Bring action hither; this cannot go to war.
A stirring dwarf we do allowance give
Before a sleeping giant. Tell him so.

PATROCLUS.

I shall, and bring his answer presently.

[Exit.]

AGAMEMNON.

In second voice we'll not be satisfied;
We come to speak with him. Ulysses, enter you.

[Exit Ulysses.]

AJAX.

What is he more than another?

AGAMEMNON.

No more than what he thinks he is.

AJAX.

Is he so much? Do you not think he thinks himself a better man than I am?

AGAMEMNON.

No question.

AJAX.

Will you subscribe his thought and say he is?

AGAMEMNON.

No, noble Ajax; you are as strong, as valiant, as wise, no less noble, much more gentle, and altogether more tractable.

AJAX.

Why should a man be proud? How doth pride grow? I know not what pride is.

AGAMEMNON.

Your mind is the clearer, Ajax, and your virtues the fairer. He that is proud eats up himself. Pride is his own glass, his own trumpet, his own chronicle; and whatever praises itself but in the deed devours the deed in the praise.

Re-enter Ulysses.

AJAX.

I do hate a proud man as I do hate the engend'ring of toads.

NESTOR.

[Aside.] And yet he loves himself: is't not strange?

ULYSSES.

Achilles will not to the field tomorrow.

AGAMEMNON.

What's his excuse?

ULYSSES.

He doth rely on none;

But carries on the stream of his dispose,

Without observance or respect of any,

In will peculiar and in self-admission.

AGAMEMNON.

Why will he not, upon our fair request,

Untent his person and share th'air with us?

ULYSSES.

Things small as nothing, for request's sake only,

He makes important; possess'd he is with greatness,

And speaks not to himself but with a pride

That quarrels at self-breath. Imagin'd worth

Holds in his blood such swol'n and hot discourse

That 'twixt his mental and his active parts

Kingdom'd Achilles in commotion rages,

And batters down himself. What should I say?

He is so plaguy proud that the death tokens of it

Cry 'No recovery.'

AGAMEMNON.

Let Ajax go to him.
Dear lord, go you and greet him in his tent.
'Tis said he holds you well; and will be led
At your request a little from himself.

ULYSSES.

O Agamemnon, let it not be so!
We'll consecrate the steps that Ajax makes
When they go from Achilles. Shall the proud lord
That bastes his arrogance with his own seam
And never suffers matter of the world
Enter his thoughts, save such as doth revolve
And ruminate himself—shall he be worshipp'd
Of that we hold an idol more than he?
No, this thrice worthy and right valiant lord
Shall not so stale his palm, nobly acquir'd,
Nor, by my will, assubjugate his merit,
As amply titled as Achilles is,
By going to Achilles.
That were to enlard his fat-already pride,
And add more coals to Cancer when he burns
With entertaining great Hyperion.
This lord go to him! Jupiter forbid,

And say in thunder 'Achilles go to him.'

NESTOR.

[Aside.] O, this is well! He rubs the vein of him.

DIOMEDES.

[Aside.] And how his silence drinks up this applause!

AJAX.

If I go to him, with my armed fist I'll pash him o'er the face.

AGAMEMNON.

O, no, you shall not go.

AJAX.

An a' be proud with me I'll pheeze his pride.

Let me go to him.

ULYSSES.

Not for the worth that hangs upon our quarrel.

AJAX.

A paltry, insolent fellow!

NESTOR.

[Aside.] How he describes himself!

AJAX.

Can he not be sociable?

ULYSSES.

[Aside.] The raven chides blackness.

AJAX.

I'll let his humours blood.

AGAMEMNON.

[Aside.] He will be the physician that should be the patient.

AJAX.

And all men were o' my mind—

ULYSSES.

[Aside.] Wit would be out of fashion.

AJAX.

A' should not bear it so, a' should eat's words first.

Shall pride carry it?

NESTOR.

[Aside.] And 'twould, you'd carry half.

ULYSSES.

[Aside.] A' would have ten shares.

AJAX.

I will knead him, I'll make him supple.

NESTOR.

[Aside.] He's not yet through warm. Force him with praises; pour in, pour in; his ambition is dry.

ULYSSES.

[To Agamemnon.] My lord, you feed too much on this dislike.

NESTOR.

Our noble general, do not do so.

DIOMEDES.

You must prepare to fight without Achilles.

ULYSSES.

Why 'tis this naming of him does him harm.

Here is a man—but 'tis before his face;

I will be silent.

NESTOR.

Wherefore should you so?

He is not emulous, as Achilles is.

ULYSSES.

Know the whole world, he is as valiant.

AJAX.

A whoreson dog, that shall palter with us thus!

Would he were a Trojan!

NESTOR.

What a vice were it in Ajax now—

ULYSSES.

If he were proud.

DIOMEDES.

Or covetous of praise.

ULYSSES.

Ay, or surly borne.

DIOMEDES.

Or strange, or self-affected.

ULYSSES.

Thank the heavens, lord, thou art of sweet composure
Praise him that gat thee, she that gave thee suck;
Fam'd be thy tutor, and thy parts of nature
Thrice fam'd beyond, beyond all erudition;
But he that disciplin'd thine arms to fight—
Let Mars divide eternity in twain
And give him half; and, for thy vigour,
Bull-bearing Milo his addition yield
To sinewy Ajax. I will not praise thy wisdom,
Which, like a bourn, a pale, a shore, confines
Thy spacious and dilated parts. Here's Nestor,
Instructed by the antiquary times—
He must, he is, he cannot but be wise;
But pardon, father Nestor, were your days
As green as Ajax' and your brain so temper'd,
You should not have the eminence of him,
But be as Ajax.

AJAX.

Shall I call you father?

NESTOR.

Ay, my good son.

DIOMEDES.

Be rul'd by him, Lord Ajax.

ULYSSES.

There is no tarrying here; the hart Achilles
Keeps thicket. Please it our great general
To call together all his state of war;
Fresh kings are come to Troy. Tomorrow
We must with all our main of power stand fast;
And here's a lord—come knights from east to west
And cull their flower, Ajax shall cope the best.

AGAMEMNON.

Go we to council. Let Achilles sleep.
Light boats sail swift, though greater hulks draw deep.

[Exeunt.]

ACT III

SCENE I. Troy. PRIAM'S palace.

Music sounds within. Enter Pandarus and a Servant.

PANDARUS.

Friend, you—pray you, a word. Do you not follow the young Lord Paris?

SERVANT.

Ay, sir, when he goes before me.

PANDARUS.

You depend upon him, I mean?

SERVANT.

Sir, I do depend upon the Lord.

PANDARUS.

You depend upon a notable gentleman; I must needs praise him.

SERVANT.

The Lord be praised!

PANDARUS.

You know me, do you not?

SERVANT.

Faith, sir, superficially.

PANDARUS.

Friend, know me better: I am the Lord Pandarus.

SERVANT.

I hope I shall know your honour better.

PANDARUS.

I do desire it.

SERVANT.

You are in the state of grace?

PANDARUS.

Grace? Not so, friend; honour and lordship are my titles. What music is this?

SERVANT.

I do but partly know, sir; it is music in parts.

PANDARUS.

Know you the musicians?

SERVANT.

Wholly, sir.

PANDARUS.

Who play they to?

SERVANT.

To the hearers, sir.

PANDARUS.

At whose pleasure, friend?

SERVANT.

At mine, sir, and theirs that love music.

PANDARUS.

Command, I mean, friend.

SERVANT.

Who shall I command, sir?

PANDARUS.

Friend, we understand not one another: I am too courtly, and thou art too cunning. At whose request do these men play?

SERVANT.

That's to't, indeed, sir. Marry, sir, at the request of Paris my lord, who is there in person; with him the mortal Venus, the heart-blood of beauty, love's invisible soul—

PANDARUS.

Who, my cousin, Cressida?

SERVANT.

No, sir, Helen. Could not you find out that by her attributes?

PANDARUS.

It should seem, fellow, that thou hast not seen the Lady Cressida. I come to speak with Paris from the Prince Troilus; I will make a complimental assault upon him, for my business seethes.

SERVANT.

Sodden business! There's a stew'd phrase indeed!

Enter Paris and Helen, attended.

PANDARUS.

Fair be to you, my lord, and to all this fair company! Fair desires, in all fair measure, fairly guide them—especially to you, fair queen! Fair thoughts be your fair pillow.

HELEN.

Dear lord, you are full of fair words.

PANDARUS.

You speak your fair pleasure, sweet queen. Fair prince, here is good broken music.

PARIS.

You have broke it, cousin; and by my life, you shall make it whole again; you shall piece it out with a piece of your performance.

HELEN.

He is full of harmony.

PANDARUS.

Truly, lady, no.

HELEN.

O, sir—

PANDARUS.

Rude, in sooth; in good sooth, very rude.

PARIS.

Well said, my lord. Well, you say so in fits.

PANDARUS.

I have business to my lord, dear queen. My lord, will you vouchsafe me a word?

HELEN.

Nay, this shall not hedge us out. We'll hear you sing, certainly—

PANDARUS.

Well sweet queen, you are pleasant with me. But, marry, thus, my lord: my dear lord and most esteemed friend, your brother Troilus—

HELEN.

My Lord Pandarus, honey-sweet lord—

PANDARUS.

Go to, sweet queen, go to—commends himself most affectionately to you—

HELEN.

You shall not bob us out of our melody. If you do, our melancholy upon your head!

PANDARUS.

Sweet queen, sweet queen; that's a sweet queen, i' faith.

HELEN.

And to make a sweet lady sad is a sour offence.

PANDARUS.

Nay, that shall not serve your turn; that shall it not, in truth, la. Nay, I care not for such words; no, no.—And, my lord, he desires you that, if the King call for him at supper, you will make his excuse.

HELEN.

My Lord Pandarus!

PANDARUS.

What says my sweet queen, my very very sweet queen?

PARIS.

What exploit's in hand? Where sups he tonight?

HELEN.

Nay, but, my lord—

PANDARUS.

What says my sweet queen?—My cousin will fall out with you.

HELEN.

You must not know where he sups.

PARIS.

I'll lay my life, with my disposer Cressida.

PANDARUS.

No, no, no such matter; you are wide. Come, your disposer is sick.

PARIS.

Well, I'll make's excuse.

PANDARUS.

Ay, good my lord. Why should you say Cressida?

No, your poor disposer's sick.

PARIS.

I spy.

PANDARUS.

You spy! What do you spy?—Come, give me an instrument. Now, sweet queen.

HELEN.

Why, this is kindly done.

PANDARUS.

My niece is horribly in love with a thing you have, sweet queen.

HELEN.

She shall have it, my lord, if it be not my Lord Paris.

PANDARUS.

He? No, she'll none of him; they two are twain.

HELEN.

Falling in, after falling out, may make them three.

PANDARUS.

Come, come. I'll hear no more of this; I'll sing you a song now.

HELEN.

Ay, ay, prithee now. By my troth, sweet lord, thou hast a fine forehead.

PANDARUS.

Ay, you may, you may.

HELEN.

Let thy song be love. This love will undo us all. O Cupid, Cupid, Cupid!

PANDARUS.

Love! Ay, that it shall, i' faith.

PARIS.

Ay, good now, love, love, nothing but love.

PANDARUS.

In good troth, it begins so.

[Sings.]

Love, love, nothing but love, still love, still more!
For, oh, love's bow
Shoots buck and doe;
The shaft confounds
Not that it wounds,

But tickles still the sore.
These lovers cry, O ho, they die!
Yet that which seems the wound to kill
Doth turn O ho! to ha! ha! he!
So dying love lives still.
O ho! a while, but ha! ha! ha!
O ho! groans out for ha! ha! ha!—hey ho!

HELEN.

In love, i' faith, to the very tip of the nose.

PARIS.

He eats nothing but doves, love; and that breeds hot blood, and hot blood begets hot thoughts, and hot thoughts beget hot deeds, and hot deeds is love.

PANDARUS.

Is this the generation of love: hot blood, hot thoughts, and hot deeds? Why, they are vipers. Is love a generation of vipers? Sweet lord, who's a-field today?

PARIS.

Hector, Deiphobus, Helenus, Antenor, and all the gallantry of Troy. I would fain have arm'd today, but my Nell would not have it so. How chance my brother Troilus went not?

HELEN.

He hangs the lip at something. You know all, Lord Pandarus.

PANDARUS.

Not I, honey-sweet queen. I long to hear how they spend today. You'll remember your brother's excuse?

PARIS.

To a hair.

PANDARUS.

Farewell, sweet queen.

HELEN.

Commend me to your niece.

PANDARUS.

I will, sweet queen.

[Exit. Sound a retreat.]

PARIS.

They're come from the field. Let us to Priam's hall
To greet the warriors. Sweet Helen, I must woo you
To help unarm our Hector. His stubborn buckles,
With these your white enchanting fingers touch'd,
Shall more obey than to the edge of steel
Or force of Greekish sinews; you shall do more
Than all the island kings—disarm great Hector.

HELEN.

'Twill make us proud to be his servant, Paris;
Yea, what he shall receive of us in duty
Gives us more palm in beauty than we have,
Yea, overshines ourself.

PARIS.

Sweet, above thought I love thee.

[Exeunt.]

SCENE II. Troy. PANDARUS' orchard.

Enter Pandarus and Troilus' Boy, meeting.

PANDARUS.

How now! Where's thy master? At my cousin Cressida's?

BOY.

No, sir; he stays for you to conduct him thither.

Enter Troilus.

PANDARUS.

O, here he comes. How now, how now?

TROILUS.

Sirrah, walk off.

[Exit Boy.]

PANDARUS.

Have you seen my cousin?

TROILUS.

No, Pandarus. I stalk about her door

Like a strange soul upon the Stygian banks

Staying for waftage. O, be thou my Charon,

And give me swift transportance to these fields

Where I may wallow in the lily beds

Propos'd for the deserver! O gentle Pandar,

from Cupid's shoulder pluck his painted wings,

and fly with me to Cressid!

PANDARUS.

Walk here i' th' orchard, I'll bring her straight.

[Exit.]

TROILUS.

I am giddy; expectation whirls me round.

Th'imaginary relish is so sweet

That it enchants my sense; what will it be

When that the wat'ry palate tastes indeed

Love's thrice-repured nectar? Death, I fear me;

Sounding destruction; or some joy too fine,

Too subtle-potent, tun'd too sharp in sweetness,

For the capacity of my ruder powers.

I fear it much; and I do fear besides

That I shall lose distinction in my joys;

As doth a battle, when they charge on heaps

The enemy flying.

Re-enter Pandarus.

PANDARUS.

She's making her ready, she'll come straight; you must be witty now. She does so blush, and fetches her wind so short, as if she were fray'd with a sprite. I'll fetch her. It is the prettiest villain; she fetches her breath as short as a new-ta'en sparrow.

[Exit.]

TROILUS.

Even such a passion doth embrace my bosom.

My heart beats thicker than a feverous pulse,

And all my powers do their bestowing lose,

Like vassalage at unawares encount'ring

The eye of majesty.

Re-enter Pandarus with Cressida.

PANDARUS.

Come, come, what need you blush? Shame's a baby. Here she is now; swear the oaths now to her that you have sworn to me.—What, are you gone again? You must be watch'd ere you be made tame, must you? Come your ways, come your ways; and you draw backward, we'll put you i' th' fills. Why do you not speak to her? Come, draw this curtain and let's see your picture. Alas the day, how loath you are to offend daylight! And 'twere dark, you'd close sooner. So, so; rub on, and kiss the mistress. How now, a kiss in fee-farm! Build there, carpenter; the air is sweet. Nay, you shall fight your hearts out ere I part you. The falcon as the tercel, for all the ducks i' th' river. Go to, go to.

TROILUS.

You have bereft me of all words, lady.

PANDARUS.

Words pay no debts, give her deeds; but she'll bereave you o' th' deeds too, if she call your activity in question. What, billing again? Here's 'In witness whereof the parties interchangeably.' Come in, come in; I'll go get a fire.

[Exit.]

CRESSIDA.

Will you walk in, my lord?

TROILUS.

O Cressid, how often have I wish'd me thus!

CRESSIDA.

Wish'd, my lord! The gods grant—O my lord!

TROILUS.

What should they grant? What makes this pretty abruption? What too curious dreg espies my sweet lady in the fountain of our love?

CRESSIDA.

More dregs than water, if my fears have eyes.

TROILUS.

Fears make devils of cherubins; they never see truly.

CRESSIDA.

Blind fear, that seeing reason leads, finds safer footing than blind reason stumbling without fear. To fear the worst oft cures the worse.

TROILUS.

O, let my lady apprehend no fear! In all Cupid's pageant there is presented no monster.

CRESSIDA.

Nor nothing monstrous neither?

TROILUS.

Nothing, but our undertakings when we vow to weep seas, live in fire, eat rocks, tame tigers; thinking it harder for our mistress to devise imposition enough than for us to undergo any difficulty imposed. This is the monstruosity in love, lady, that the will is infinite, and the execution confin'd; that the desire is boundless, and the act a slave to limit.

CRESSIDA.

They say all lovers swear more performance than they are able, and yet reserve an ability that they never perform; vowing more than the perfection of ten, and discharging less than the tenth part of one. They that have the voice of lions and the act of hares, are they not monsters?

TROILUS.

Are there such? Such are not we. Praise us as we are tasted, allow us as we prove; our head shall go bare till merit crown it. No perfection in reversion shall have a praise in present. We will not name desert before his birth; and, being born, his addition shall be humble. Few words to fair faith: Troilus shall be such to Cressid as what envy can say worst shall be a mock for his truth; and what truth can speak truest not truer than Troilus.

CRESSIDA.

Will you walk in, my lord?

Re-enter Pandarus.

PANDARUS.

What, blushing still? Have you not done talking yet?

CRESSIDA.

Well, uncle, what folly I commit, I dedicate to you.

PANDARUS.

I thank you for that; if my lord get a boy of you, you'll give him me. Be true to my lord; if he flinch, chide me for it.

TROILUS.

You know now your hostages: your uncle's word and my firm faith.

PANDARUS.

Nay, I'll give my word for her too: our kindred, though they be long ere they are wooed, they are constant being won; they are burs, I can tell you; they'll stick where they are thrown.

CRESSIDA.

Boldness comes to me now and brings me heart.

Prince Troilus, I have lov'd you night and day

For many weary months.

TROILUS.

Why was my Cressid then so hard to win?

CRESSIDA.

Hard to seem won; but I was won, my lord,

With the first glance that ever—pardon me.

If I confess much, you will play the tyrant.

I love you now; but till now not so much

But I might master it. In faith, I lie;

My thoughts were like unbridled children, grown

Too headstrong for their mother. See, we fools!

Why have I blabb'd? Who shall be true to us,

When we are so unsecret to ourselves?

But, though I lov'd you well, I woo'd you not;

And yet, good faith, I wish'd myself a man,

Or that we women had men's privilege

Of speaking first. Sweet, bid me hold my tongue,

For in this rapture I shall surely speak

The thing I shall repent. See, see, your silence,

Cunning in dumbness, from my weakness draws

My very soul of counsel. Stop my mouth.

TROILUS.

And shall, albeit sweet music issues thence.

PANDARUS.

Pretty, i' faith.

CRESSIDA.

My lord, I do beseech you, pardon me;

'Twas not my purpose thus to beg a kiss.

I am asham'd. O heavens! what have I done?

For this time will I take my leave, my lord.

TROILUS.

Your leave, sweet Cressid!

PANDARUS.

Leave! And you take leave till tomorrow morning—

CRESSIDA.

Pray you, content you.

TROILUS.

What offends you, lady?

CRESSIDA.

Sir, mine own company.

TROILUS.

You cannot shun yourself.

CRESSIDA.

Let me go and try.

I have a kind of self resides with you;

But an unkind self, that itself will leave

To be another's fool. I would be gone.

Where is my wit? I know not what I speak.

TROILUS.

Well know they what they speak that speak so wisely.

CRESSIDA.

Perchance, my lord, I show more craft than love;

And fell so roundly to a large confession

To angle for your thoughts; but you are wise—

Or else you love not; for to be wise and love

Exceeds man's might; that dwells with gods above.

TROILUS.

O that I thought it could be in a woman—

As, if it can, I will presume in you—

To feed for aye her lamp and flames of love;

To keep her constancy in plight and youth,

Outliving beauty's outward, with a mind

That doth renew swifter than blood decays!

Or that persuasion could but thus convince me

That my integrity and truth to you

Might be affronted with the match and weight

Of such a winnowed purity in love.

How were I then uplifted! But, alas,

I am as true as truth's simplicity,

And simpler than the infancy of truth.

CRESSIDA.

In that I'll war with you.

TROILUS.

O virtuous fight,

When right with right wars who shall be most right!

True swains in love shall in the world to come

Approve their truth by Troilus, when their rhymes,

Full of protest, of oath, and big compare,

Want similes, truth tir'd with iteration—

As true as steel, as plantage to the moon,

As sun to day, as turtle to her mate,

As iron to adamant, as earth to th' centre—

Yet, after all comparisons of truth,

As truth's authentic author to be cited,

'As true as Troilus' shall crown up the verse

And sanctify the numbers.

CRESSIDA.

Prophet may you be!

If I be false, or swerve a hair from truth,

When time is old and hath forgot itself,

When waterdrops have worn the stones of Troy,

And blind oblivion swallow'd cities up,
And mighty states characterless are grated
To dusty nothing—yet let memory
From false to false, among false maids in love,
Upbraid my falsehood when th' have said 'As false
As air, as water, wind, or sandy earth,
As fox to lamb, or wolf to heifer's calf,
Pard to the hind, or stepdame to her son'—
Yea, let them say, to stick the heart of falsehood,
'As false as Cressid.'

PANDARUS.

Go to, a bargain made; seal it, seal it; I'll be the witness. Here I hold your hand; here my cousin's. If ever you prove false one to another, since I have taken such pains to bring you together, let all pitiful goers-between be call'd to the world's end after my name—call them all Pandars; let all constant men be Troiluses, all false women Cressids, and all brokers between Pandars. Say 'Amen.'

TROILUS.

Amen.

CRESSIDA.

Amen.

PANDARUS.

Amen. Whereupon I will show you a chamber and a bed; which bed, because it shall not speak of your pretty encounters, press it to death. Away!

[Exeunt Troilus and Cressida.]

And Cupid grant all tongue-tied maidens here,

Bed, chamber, pander, to provide this gear!

[Exit.]

SCENE III. The Greek camp.

Flourish. Enter Agamemnon, Ulysses, Diomedes, Nestor, Ajax, Menelaus and Calchas.

CALCHAS.

Now, Princes, for the service I have done,

Th'advantage of the time prompts me aloud

To call for recompense. Appear it to your mind

That, through the sight I bear in things to come,

I have abandon'd Troy, left my possession,

Incurr'd a traitor's name, expos'd myself

From certain and possess'd conveniences

To doubtful fortunes, sequest'ring from me all

That time, acquaintance, custom, and condition,

Made tame and most familiar to my nature;

And here, to do you service, am become

As new into the world, strange, unacquainted—

I do beseech you, as in way of taste,

To give me now a little benefit

Out of those many regist'red in promise,

Which you say live to come in my behalf.

AGAMEMNON.

What wouldst thou of us, Trojan? Make demand.

CALCHAS.

You have a Trojan prisoner call'd Antenor,
Yesterday took; Troy holds him very dear.
Oft have you—often have you thanks therefore—
Desir'd my Cressid in right great exchange,
Whom Troy hath still denied; but this Antenor,
I know, is such a wrest in their affairs
That their negotiations all must slack
Wanting his manage; and they will almost
Give us a prince of blood, a son of Priam,
In change of him. Let him be sent, great Princes,
And he shall buy my daughter; and her presence
Shall quite strike off all service I have done
In most accepted pain.

AGAMEMNON.

Let Diomedes bear him,
And bring us Cressid hither. Calchas shall have
What he requests of us. Good Diomed,
Furnish you fairly for this interchange;
Withal, bring word if Hector will tomorrow
Be answer'd in his challenge. Ajax is ready.

DIOMEDES.

This shall I undertake; and 'tis a burden

Which I am proud to bear.

[Exeunt Diomedes and Calchas.]

[Achilles and Patroclus stand in their tent.]

ULYSSES.

Achilles stands i' th'entrance of his tent.
Please it our general pass strangely by him,
As if he were forgot; and, Princes all,
Lay negligent and loose regard upon him.
I will come last. 'Tis like he'll question me
Why such unplausive eyes are bent, why turn'd on him.
If so, I have derision med'cinable
To use between your strangeness and his pride,
Which his own will shall have desire to drink.
It may do good. Pride hath no other glass
To show itself but pride; for supple knees
Feed arrogance and are the proud man's fees.

AGAMEMNON.

We'll execute your purpose, and put on
A form of strangeness as we pass along.
So do each lord; and either greet him not,
Or else disdainfully, which shall shake him more
Than if not look'd on. I will lead the way.

ACHILLES.

What comes the general to speak with me?

You know my mind. I'll fight no more 'gainst Troy.

AGAMEMNON.

What says Achilles? Would he aught with us?

NESTOR.

Would you, my lord, aught with the general?

ACHILLES.

No.

NESTOR.

Nothing, my lord.

AGAMEMNON.

The better.

[Exeunt Agamemnon and Nestor.]

ACHILLES.

Good day, good day.

MENELAUS.

How do you? How do you?

[Exit.]

ACHILLES.

What, does the cuckold scorn me?

AJAX.

How now, Patroclus?

ACHILLES.

Good morrow, Ajax.

AJAX.

Ha?

ACHILLES.

Good morrow.

AJAX.

Ay, and good next day too.

[Exit.]

ACHILLES.

What mean these fellows? Know they not Achilles?

PATROCLUS.

They pass by strangely. They were us'd to bend,
To send their smiles before them to Achilles,
To come as humbly as they us'd to creep
To holy altars.

ACHILLES.

What, am I poor of late?
'Tis certain, greatness, once fall'n out with fortune,
Must fall out with men too. What the declin'd is,
He shall as soon read in the eyes of others
As feel in his own fall; for men, like butterflies,
Show not their mealy wings but to the summer;
And not a man for being simply man
Hath any honour, but honour for those honours
That are without him, as place, riches, and favour,
Prizes of accident, as oft as merit;

Which when they fall, as being slippery standers,
The love that lean'd on them as slippery too,
Doth one pluck down another, and together
Die in the fall. But 'tis not so with me:
Fortune and I are friends; I do enjoy
At ample point all that I did possess
Save these men's looks; who do, methinks, find out
Something not worth in me such rich beholding
As they have often given. Here is Ulysses.
I'll interrupt his reading.
How now, Ulysses!

ULYSSES.

Now, great Thetis' son!

ACHILLES.

What are you reading?

ULYSSES.

A strange fellow here
Writes me that man—how dearly ever parted,
How much in having, or without or in—
Cannot make boast to have that which he hath,
Nor feels not what he owes, but by reflection;
As when his virtues shining upon others
Heat them, and they retort that heat again

To the first giver.

ACHILLES.

This is not strange, Ulysses.

The beauty that is borne here in the face

The bearer knows not, but commends itself

To others' eyes; nor doth the eye itself—

That most pure spirit of sense—behold itself,

Not going from itself; but eye to eye opposed

Salutes each other with each other's form;

For speculation turns not to itself

Till it hath travell'd, and is mirror'd there

Where it may see itself. This is not strange at all.

ULYSSES.

I do not strain at the position—

It is familiar—but at the author's drift;

Who, in his circumstance, expressly proves

That no man is the lord of anything,

Though in and of him there be much consisting,

Till he communicate his parts to others;

Nor doth he of himself know them for aught

Till he behold them formed in the applause

Where th'are extended; who, like an arch, reverb'rate

The voice again; or, like a gate of steel

Fronting the sun, receives and renders back
His figure and his heat. I was much rapt in this;
And apprehended here immediately
Th'unknown Ajax. Heavens, what a man is there!
A very horse that has he knows not what!
Nature, what things there are
Most abject in regard and dear in use!
What things again most dear in the esteem
And poor in worth! Now shall we see tomorrow—
An act that very chance doth throw upon him—
Ajax renown'd. O heavens, what some men do,
While some men leave to do!
How some men creep in skittish Fortune's hall,
Whiles others play the idiots in her eyes!
How one man eats into another's pride,
While pride is fasting in his wantonness!
To see these Grecian lords!—why, even already
They clap the lubber Ajax on the shoulder,
As if his foot were on brave Hector's breast,
And great Troy shrieking.

ACHILLES.

I do believe it; for they pass'd by me
As misers do by beggars, neither gave to me

Good word nor look. What, are my deeds forgot?

ULYSSES.

Time hath, my lord, a wallet at his back,
Wherein he puts alms for oblivion,
A great-siz'd monster of ingratitudes.
Those scraps are good deeds past, which are devour'd
As fast as they are made, forgot as soon
As done. Perseverance, dear my lord,
Keeps honour bright. To have done is to hang
Quite out of fashion, like a rusty mail
In monumental mock'ry. Take the instant way;
For honour travels in a strait so narrow—
Where one but goes abreast. Keep then the path,
For emulation hath a thousand sons
That one by one pursue; if you give way,
Or hedge aside from the direct forthright,
Like to an ent'red tide they all rush by
And leave you hindmost;
Or, like a gallant horse fall'n in first rank,
Lie there for pavement to the abject rear,
O'er-run and trampled on. Then what they do in present,
Though less than yours in past, must o'ertop yours;
For Time is like a fashionable host,

That slightly shakes his parting guest by th'hand;
And with his arms out-stretch'd, as he would fly,
Grasps in the comer. The welcome ever smiles,
And farewell goes out sighing. O, let not virtue seek
Remuneration for the thing it was;
For beauty, wit,
High birth, vigour of bone, desert in service,
Love, friendship, charity, are subjects all
To envious and calumniating Time.
One touch of nature makes the whole world kin—
That all with one consent praise new-born gauds,
Though they are made and moulded of things past,
And give to dust that is a little gilt
More laud than gilt o'er-dusted.
The present eye praises the present object.
Then marvel not, thou great and complete man,
That all the Greeks begin to worship Ajax,
Since things in motion sooner catch the eye
Than what stirs not. The cry went once on thee,
And still it might, and yet it may again,
If thou wouldst not entomb thyself alive
And case thy reputation in thy tent,
Whose glorious deeds but in these fields of late

Made emulous missions 'mongst the gods themselves,

And drave great Mars to faction.

ACHILLES.

Of this my privacy

I have strong reasons.

ULYSSES.

But 'gainst your privacy

The reasons are more potent and heroical.

'Tis known, Achilles, that you are in love

With one of Priam's daughters.

ACHILLES.

Ha! known!

ULYSSES.

Is that a wonder?

The providence that's in a watchful state

Knows almost every grain of Plutus' gold;

Finds bottom in th'uncomprehensive deeps;

Keeps place with thought, and almost, like the gods,

Do thoughts unveil in their dumb cradles.

There is a mystery—with whom relation

Durst never meddle—in the soul of state,

Which hath an operation more divine

Than breath or pen can give expressure to.

All the commerce that you have had with Troy
As perfectly is ours as yours, my lord;
And better would it fit Achilles much
To throw down Hector than Polyxena.
But it must grieve young Pyrrhus now at home,
When fame shall in our island sound her trump,
And all the Greekish girls shall tripping sing
'Great Hector's sister did Achilles win;
But our great Ajax bravely beat down him.'
Farewell, my lord. I as your lover speak.
The fool slides o'er the ice that you should break.

[Exit.]

PATROCLUS.

To this effect, Achilles, have I mov'd you.
A woman impudent and mannish grown
Is not more loath'd than an effeminate man
In time of action. I stand condemn'd for this;
They think my little stomach to the war
And your great love to me restrains you thus.
Sweet, rouse yourself; and the weak wanton Cupid
Shall from your neck unloose his amorous fold,
And, like a dew-drop from the lion's mane,
Be shook to air.

ACHILLES.

Shall Ajax fight with Hector?

PATROCLUS.

Ay, and perhaps receive much honour by him.

ACHILLES.

I see my reputation is at stake;

My fame is shrewdly gor'd.

PATROCLUS.

O, then, beware:

Those wounds heal ill that men do give themselves;

Omission to do what is necessary

Seals a commission to a blank of danger;

And danger, like an ague, subtly taints

Even then when they sit idly in the sun.

ACHILLES.

Go call Thersites hither, sweet Patroclus.

I'll send the fool to Ajax, and desire him

T'invite the Trojan lords, after the combat,

To see us here unarm'd. I have a woman's longing,

An appetite that I am sick withal,

To see great Hector in his weeds of peace;

To talk with him, and to behold his visage,

Even to my full of view.

Enter Thersites.

A labour sav'd!

THERSITES.

A wonder!

ACHILLES.

What?

THERSITES.

Ajax goes up and down the field asking for himself.

ACHILLES.

How so?

THERSITES.

He must fight singly tomorrow with Hector, and is so prophetically proud of an heroical cudgelling that he raves in saying nothing.

ACHILLES.

How can that be?

THERSITES.

Why, a' stalks up and down like a peacock—a stride and a stand; ruminates like an hostess that hath no arithmetic but her brain to set down her reckoning, bites his lip with a politic regard, as who should say 'There were wit in this head, and 'twould out'; and so there is; but it lies as coldly in him as fire in a flint, which will not show without knocking. The man's undone for ever; for if Hector break not his neck i' th' combat, he'll break't himself in vainglory. He knows not me. I said 'Good morrow, Ajax'; and he replies 'Thanks, Agamemnon.' What think you of this man that takes me for the general? He's grown a very land fish, languageless, a monster. A plague of opinion! A man may wear it on both sides, like leather jerkin.

ACHILLES.

Thou must be my ambassador to him, Thersites.

THERSITES.

Who, I? Why, he'll answer nobody; he professes not answering. Speaking is for beggars: he wears his tongue in's arms. I will put on his presence. Let Patroclus make his demands to me, you shall see the pageant of Ajax.

ACHILLES.

To him, Patroclus. Tell him I humbly desire the valiant Ajax to invite the most valorous Hector to come unarm'd to my tent; and to procure safe conduct for his person of the magnanimous and most illustrious six-or-seven-times-honour'd Captain General of the Grecian army, Agamemnon. Do this.

PATROCLUS.

Jove bless great Ajax!

THERSITES.

Hum!

PATROCLUS.

I come from the worthy Achilles—

THERSITES.

Ha!

PATROCLUS.

Who most humbly desires you to invite Hector to his tent—

THERSITES.

Hum!

PATROCLUS.

And to procure safe conduct from Agamemnon.

THERSITES.

Agamemnon?

PATROCLUS.

Ay, my lord.

THERSITES.

Ha!

PATROCLUS.

What you say to't?

THERSITES.

God buy you, with all my heart.

PATROCLUS.

Your answer, sir.

THERSITES.

If tomorrow be a fair day, by eleven of the clock it will go one way or other. Howsoever, he shall pay for me ere he has me.

PATROCLUS.

Your answer, sir.

THERSITES.

Fare ye well, with all my heart.

ACHILLES.

Why, but he is not in this tune, is he?

THERSITES.

No, but out of tune thus. What music will be in him when Hector has knock'd out his brains, I know not; but, I am sure, none; unless the fiddler Apollo get his sinews to make catlings on.

ACHILLES.

Come, thou shalt bear a letter to him straight.

THERSITES.

Let me bear another to his horse; for that's the more capable creature.

ACHILLES.

My mind is troubled, like a fountain stirr'd;

And I myself see not the bottom of it.

[Exeunt Achilles and Patroclus.]

THERSITES.

Would the fountain of your mind were clear again, that I might water an ass at it. I had rather be a tick in a sheep than such a valiant ignorance.

[Exit.]

ACT IV

SCENE I. Troy. A street.

Enter, at one side, Aeneas and servant with a torch; at another Paris, Deiphobus, Antenor, Diomedes the Grecian, and others, with torches.

PARIS.

See, ho! Who is that there?

DEIPHOBUS.

It is the Lord Aeneas.

AENEAS.

Is the Prince there in person?

Had I so good occasion to lie long

As you, Prince Paris, nothing but heavenly business

Should rob my bed-mate of my company.

DIOMEDES.

That's my mind too. Good morrow, Lord Aeneas.

PARIS.

A valiant Greek, Aeneas—take his hand:

Witness the process of your speech, wherein

You told how Diomed, a whole week by days,

Did haunt you in the field.

AENEAS.

Health to you, valiant sir,

During all question of the gentle truce;

But when I meet you arm'd, as black defiance

As heart can think or courage execute.

DIOMEDES.

The one and other Diomed embraces.

Our bloods are now in calm; and so long health!

But when contention and occasion meet,

By Jove, I'll play the hunter for thy life

With all my force, pursuit, and policy.

AENEAS.

And thou shalt hunt a lion that will fly

With his face backward. In humane gentleness,

Welcome to Troy! Now, by Anchises' life,

Welcome indeed! By Venus' hand I swear

No man alive can love in such a sort

The thing he means to kill, more excellently.

DIOMEDES.

We sympathise. Jove let Aeneas live,

If to my sword his fate be not the glory,

A thousand complete courses of the sun!

But in mine emulous honour let him die

With every joint a wound, and that tomorrow!

AENEAS.

We know each other well.

DIOMEDES.

We do; and long to know each other worse.

PARIS.

This is the most despiteful gentle greeting

The noblest hateful love, that e'er I heard of.

What business, lord, so early?

AENEAS.

I was sent for to the King; but why, I know not.

PARIS.

His purpose meets you: 'twas to bring this Greek

To Calchas' house, and there to render him,

For the enfreed Antenor, the fair Cressid.

Let's have your company; or, if you please,

Haste there before us. I constantly believe—

Or rather call my thought a certain knowledge—

My brother Troilus lodges there tonight.

Rouse him and give him note of our approach,

With the whole quality wherefore; I fear

We shall be much unwelcome.

AENEAS.

That I assure you:

Troilus had rather Troy were borne to Greece

Than Cressid borne from Troy.

PARIS.

There is no help;

The bitter disposition of the time

Will have it so. On, lord; we'll follow you.

AENEAS.

Good morrow, all.

[Exit with servant.]

PARIS.

And tell me, noble Diomed, faith, tell me true,

Even in the soul of sound good-fellowship,

Who in your thoughts deserves fair Helen best,

Myself, or Menelaus?

DIOMEDES.

Both alike:

He merits well to have her that doth seek her,

Not making any scruple of her soilure,

With such a hell of pain and world of charge;

And you as well to keep her that defend her,

Not palating the taste of her dishonour,

With such a costly loss of wealth and friends.

He like a puling cuckold would drink up

The lees and dregs of a flat tamed piece;

You, like a lecher, out of whorish loins

Are pleas'd to breed out your inheritors.

Both merits pois'd, each weighs nor less nor more,

But he as he, the heavier for a whore.

PARIS.

You are too bitter to your country-woman.

DIOMEDES.

She's bitter to her country. Hear me, Paris:

For every false drop in her bawdy veins

A Grecian's life hath sunk; for every scruple

Of her contaminated carrion weight

A Trojan hath been slain. Since she could speak,

She hath not given so many good words breath

As for her Greeks and Trojans suff'red death.

PARIS.

Fair Diomed, you do as chapmen do,

Dispraise the thing that you desire to buy;

But we in silence hold this virtue well,

We'll not commend what we intend to sell.

Here lies our way.

[Exeunt.]

SCENE II. Troy. The court of PANDARUS' house.

Enter Troilus and Cressida.

TROILUS.

Dear, trouble not yourself; the morn is cold.

CRESSIDA.

Then, sweet my lord, I'll call mine uncle down;

He shall unbolt the gates.

TROILUS.

Trouble him not;

To bed, to bed! Sleep kill those pretty eyes,

And give as soft attachment to thy senses

As infants empty of all thought!

CRESSIDA.

Good morrow, then.

TROILUS.

I prithee now, to bed.

CRESSIDA.

Are you aweary of me?

TROILUS.

O Cressida! but that the busy day,

Wak'd by the lark, hath rous'd the ribald crows,

And dreaming night will hide our joys no longer,

I would not from thee.

CRESSIDA.

Night hath been too brief.

TROILUS.

Beshrew the witch! with venomous wights she stays

As tediously as hell, but flies the grasps of love

With wings more momentary-swift than thought.

You will catch cold, and curse me.

CRESSIDA.

Prithee tarry.

You men will never tarry.

O foolish Cressid! I might have still held off,

And then you would have tarried. Hark! there's one up.

PANDARUS.

[Within.] What's all the doors open here?

TROILUS.

It is your uncle.

Enter Pandarus.

CRESSIDA.

A pestilence on him! Now will he be mocking.

I shall have such a life!

PANDARUS.

How now, how now! How go maidenheads?

Here, you maid! Where's my cousin Cressid?

CRESSIDA.

Go hang yourself, you naughty mocking uncle.

You bring me to do, and then you flout me too.

PANDARUS.

To do what? to do what? Let her say what.

What have I brought you to do?

CRESSIDA.

Come, come, beshrew your heart! You'll ne'er be good, nor suffer others.

PANDARUS.

Ha, ha! Alas, poor wretch! Ah, poor capocchia! Hast not slept tonight? Would he not, a naughty man, let it sleep? A bugbear take him!

CRESSIDA.

Did not I tell you? Would he were knock'd i' th' head!

[One knocks.]

Who's that at door? Good uncle, go and see.

My lord, come you again into my chamber.

You smile and mock me, as if I meant naughtily.

TROILUS.

Ha! ha!

CRESSIDA.

Come, you are deceiv'd, I think of no such thing.

[Knock.]

How earnestly they knock! Pray you come in:

I would not for half Troy have you seen here.

[Exeunt Troilus and Cressida.]

PANDARUS.

Who's there? What's the matter? Will you beat down the door? How now? What's the matter?

Enter Aeneas.

AENEAS.

Good morrow, lord, good morrow.

PANDARUS.

Who's there? My lord Aeneas? By my troth,

I knew you not. What news with you so early?

AENEAS.

Is not Prince Troilus here?

PANDARUS.

Here! What should he do here?

AENEAS.

Come, he is here, my lord; do not deny him.

It doth import him much to speak with me.

PANDARUS.

Is he here, say you? It's more than I know, I'll be sworn. For my own part, I came in late. What should he do here?

AENEAS.

Who, nay then! Come, come, you'll do him wrong ere you are ware; you'll be so true to him to be false to him. Do not you know of him, but yet go fetch him hither; go.

Re-enter Troilus.

TROILUS.

How now! What's the matter?

AENEAS.

My lord, I scarce have leisure to salute you,
My matter is so rash. There is at hand
Paris your brother, and Deiphobus,
The Grecian Diomed, and our Antenor
Deliver'd to us; and for him forthwith,
Ere the first sacrifice, within this hour,
We must give up to Diomedes' hand
The Lady Cressida.

TROILUS.

Is it so concluded?

AENEAS.

By Priam and the general state of Troy.
They are at hand, and ready to effect it.

TROILUS.

How my achievements mock me!
I will go meet them; and, my Lord Aeneas,
We met by chance; you did not find me here.

AENEAS.

Good, good, my lord, the secrets of neighbour Pandar
Have not more gift in taciturnity.

[Exeunt Troilus and Aeneas.]

PANDARUS.

Is't possible? No sooner got but lost? The devil take Antenor! The young prince will go mad. A plague upon Antenor! I would they had broke's neck.

Re-enter Cressida.

CRESSIDA.

How now! What's the matter? Who was here?

PANDARUS.

Ah, ah!

CRESSIDA.

Why sigh you so profoundly? Where's my lord? Gone? Tell me, sweet uncle, what's the matter?

PANDARUS.

Would I were as deep under the earth as I am above!

CRESSIDA.

O the gods! What's the matter?

PANDARUS.

Pray thee get thee in. Would thou hadst ne'er been born! I knew thou wouldst be his death! O, poor gentleman! A plague upon Antenor!

CRESSIDA.

Good uncle, I beseech you, on my knees I beseech you, what's the matter?

PANDARUS.

Thou must be gone, wench, thou must be gone; thou art chang'd for Antenor; thou must to thy father, and be gone from Troilus. 'Twill be his death; 'twill be his bane; he cannot bear it.

CRESSIDA.

O you immortal gods! I will not go.

PANDARUS.

Thou must.

CRESSIDA.

I will not, uncle. I have forgot my father;
I know no touch of consanguinity,
No kin, no love, no blood, no soul so near me
As the sweet Troilus. O you gods divine,
Make Cressid's name the very crown of falsehood,
If ever she leave Troilus! Time, force, and death,
Do to this body what extremes you can,
But the strong base and building of my love
Is as the very centre of the earth,
Drawing all things to it. I'll go in and weep—

PANDARUS.

Do, do.

CRESSIDA.

Tear my bright hair, and scratch my praised cheeks,
Crack my clear voice with sobs and break my heart,
With sounding 'Troilus.' I will not go from Troy.

[Exeunt.]

SCENE III. Troy. A street before PANDARUS' house.

Enter Paris, Troilus, Aeneas, Deiphobus, Antenor and Diomedes.

PARIS.

It is great morning; and the hour prefix'd

For her delivery to this valiant Greek

Comes fast upon. Good my brother Troilus,

Tell you the lady what she is to do

And haste her to the purpose.

TROILUS.

Walk into her house.

I'll bring her to the Grecian presently;

And to his hand when I deliver her,

Think it an altar, and thy brother Troilus

A priest, there off'ring to it his own heart.

[Exit.]

PARIS.

I know what 'tis to love,

And would, as I shall pity, I could help!

Please you walk in, my lords?

[Exeunt.]

SCENE IV. Troy. PANDARUS' house.

Enter Pandarus and Cressida.

PANDARUS.

Be moderate, be moderate.

CRESSIDA.

Why tell you me of moderation?

The grief is fine, full, perfect, that I taste,

And violenteth in a sense as strong

As that which causeth it. How can I moderate it?

If I could temporize with my affections

Or brew it to a weak and colder palate,

The like allayment could I give my grief.

My love admits no qualifying dross;

No more my grief, in such a precious loss.

Enter Troilus.

PANDARUS.

Here, here, here he comes. Ah, sweet ducks!

CRESSIDA.

[Embracing him.] O Troilus! Troilus!

PANDARUS.

What a pair of spectacles is here! Let me embrace too. 'O heart,' as the goodly saying is,—

O heart, heavy heart,

Why sigh'st thou without breaking?

where he answers again

Because thou canst not ease thy smart

By friendship nor by speaking.

There was never a truer rhyme. Let us cast away nothing, for we may live to have need of such a verse. We see it, we see it. How now, lambs!

TROILUS.

Cressid, I love thee in so strain'd a purity

That the bless'd gods, as angry with my fancy,

More bright in zeal than the devotion which

Cold lips blow to their deities, take thee from me.

CRESSIDA.

Have the gods envy?

PANDARUS.

Ay, ay, ay, ay; 'tis too plain a case.

CRESSIDA.

And is it true that I must go from Troy?

TROILUS.

A hateful truth.

CRESSIDA.

What! and from Troilus too?

TROILUS.

From Troy and Troilus.

CRESSIDA.

Is't possible?

TROILUS.

And suddenly; where injury of chance
Puts back leave-taking, justles roughly by
All time of pause, rudely beguiles our lips
Of all rejoindure, forcibly prevents
Our lock'd embrasures, strangles our dear vows
Even in the birth of our own labouring breath.
We two, that with so many thousand sighs
Did buy each other, must poorly sell ourselves
With the rude brevity and discharge of one.
Injurious time now with a robber's haste
Crams his rich thiev'ry up, he knows not how.
As many farewells as be stars in heaven,
With distinct breath and consign'd kisses to them,
He fumbles up into a loose adieu,
And scants us with a single famish'd kiss,
Distasted with the salt of broken tears.

AENEAS.

[Within.] My lord, is the lady ready?

TROILUS.

Hark! you are call'd. Some say the Genius
Cries so to him that instantly must die.

Bid them have patience; she shall come anon.

PANDARUS.

Where are my tears? Rain, to lay this wind, or my heart will be blown up by my throat!

[Exit.]

CRESSIDA.

I must then to the Grecians?

TROILUS.

No remedy.

CRESSIDA.

A woeful Cressid 'mongst the merry Greeks!

When shall we see again?

TROILUS.

Hear me, my love. Be thou but true of heart.

CRESSIDA.

I true? How now! What wicked deem is this?

TROILUS.

Nay, we must use expostulation kindly,

For it is parting from us.

I speak not 'Be thou true' as fearing thee,

For I will throw my glove to Death himself

That there's no maculation in thy heart;

But 'Be thou true' say I to fashion in

My sequent protestation: be thou true,

And I will see thee.

CRESSIDA.

O! you shall be expos'd, my lord, to dangers

As infinite as imminent! But I'll be true.

TROILUS.

And I'll grow friend with danger. Wear this sleeve.

CRESSIDA.

And you this glove. When shall I see you?

TROILUS.

I will corrupt the Grecian sentinels

To give thee nightly visitation.

But yet be true.

CRESSIDA.

O heavens! 'Be true' again!

TROILUS.

Hear why I speak it, love.

The Grecian youths are full of quality;

They're loving, well compos'd, with gifts of nature,

Flowing and swelling o'er with arts and exercise.

How novelty may move, and parts with person,

Alas, a kind of godly jealousy,

Which, I beseech you, call a virtuous sin,

Makes me afear'd.

CRESSIDA.

O heavens! you love me not!

TROILUS.

Die I a villain then!

In this I do not call your faith in question

So mainly as my merit. I cannot sing,

Nor heel the high lavolt, nor sweeten talk,

Nor play at subtle games; fair virtues all,

To which the Grecians are most prompt and pregnant;

But I can tell that in each grace of these

There lurks a still and dumb-discoursive devil

That tempts most cunningly. But be not tempted.

CRESSIDA.

Do you think I will?

TROILUS.

No.

But something may be done that we will not;

And sometimes we are devils to ourselves,

When we will tempt the frailty of our powers,

Presuming on their changeful potency.

AENEAS.

[Within.] Nay, good my lord!

TROILUS.

Come, kiss; and let us part.

PARIS.

[Within.] Brother Troilus!

TROILUS.

Good brother, come you hither;

And bring Aeneas and the Grecian with you.

CRESSIDA.

My lord, will you be true?

TROILUS.

Who, I? Alas, it is my vice, my fault!

Whiles others fish with craft for great opinion,

I with great truth catch mere simplicity;

Whilst some with cunning gild their copper crowns,

With truth and plainness I do wear mine bare.

Fear not my truth: the moral of my wit

Is plain and true; there's all the reach of it.

Enter Aeneas, Paris, Antenor, Deiphobus and Diomedes.

Welcome, Sir Diomed! Here is the lady

Which for Antenor we deliver you;

At the port, lord, I'll give her to thy hand,

And by the way possess thee what she is.

Entreat her fair; and, by my soul, fair Greek,

If e'er thou stand at mercy of my sword,

Name Cressid, and thy life shall be as safe

As Priam is in Ilion.

DIOMEDES.

Fair Lady Cressid,

So please you, save the thanks this prince expects.

The lustre in your eye, heaven in your cheek,

Pleads your fair usage; and to Diomed

You shall be mistress, and command him wholly.

TROILUS.

Grecian, thou dost not use me courteously

To shame the zeal of my petition to thee

In praising her. I tell thee, lord of Greece,

She is as far high-soaring o'er thy praises

As thou unworthy to be call'd her servant.

I charge thee use her well, even for my charge;

For, by the dreadful Pluto, if thou dost not,

Though the great bulk Achilles be thy guard,

I'll cut thy throat.

DIOMEDES.

O, be not mov'd, Prince Troilus.

Let me be privileg'd by my place and message

To be a speaker free: when I am hence

I'll answer to my lust. And know you, lord,

I'll nothing do on charge: to her own worth

She shall be priz'd. But that you say 'Be't so,'

I speak it in my spirit and honour, 'No.'

TROILUS.

Come, to the port. I'll tell thee, Diomed,

This brave shall oft make thee to hide thy head.

Lady, give me your hand; and, as we walk,

To our own selves bend we our needful talk.

[Exeunt Troilus, Cressida and Diomedes.]

[Sound trumpet.]

PARIS.

Hark! Hector's trumpet.

AENEAS.

How have we spent this morning!

The Prince must think me tardy and remiss,

That swore to ride before him to the field.

PARIS.

'Tis Troilus' fault. Come, come to field with him.

DEIPHOBUS.

Let us make ready straight.

AENEAS.

Yea, with a bridegroom's fresh alacrity

Let us address to tend on Hector's heels.

The glory of our Troy doth this day lie

On his fair worth and single chivalry.

[Exeunt.]

SCENE V. The Grecian camp. Lists set out.

Enter Ajax, armed; Agamemnon, Achilles, Patroclus, Menelaus, Ulysses, Nestor and others.

AGAMEMNON.

Here art thou in appointment fresh and fair,

Anticipating time with starting courage.

Give with thy trumpet a loud note to Troy,

Thou dreadful Ajax, that the appalled air

May pierce the head of the great combatant,

And hale him hither.

AJAX.

Thou, trumpet, there's my purse.

Now crack thy lungs and split thy brazen pipe;

Blow, villain, till thy sphered bias cheek

Out-swell the colic of puff'd Aquilon.

Come, stretch thy chest, and let thy eyes spout blood:

Thou blowest for Hector.

[Trumpet sounds.]

ULYSSES.

No trumpet answers.

ACHILLES.

'Tis but early days.

AGAMEMNON.

Is not yond Diomed, with Calchas' daughter?

ULYSSES.

'Tis he, I ken the manner of his gait:

He rises on the toe. That spirit of his

In aspiration lifts him from the earth.

Enter Diomedes and Cressida.

AGAMEMNON.

Is this the Lady Cressid?

DIOMEDES.

Even she.

AGAMEMNON.

Most dearly welcome to the Greeks, sweet lady.

NESTOR.

Our general doth salute you with a kiss.

ULYSSES.

Yet is the kindness but particular;

'Twere better she were kiss'd in general.

NESTOR.

And very courtly counsel: I'll begin.

So much for Nestor.

ACHILLES.

I'll take that winter from your lips, fair lady.

Achilles bids you welcome.

MENELAUS.

I had good argument for kissing once.

PATROCLUS.

But that's no argument for kissing now;

For thus popp'd Paris in his hardiment,

And parted thus you and your argument.

ULYSSES.

O deadly gall, and theme of all our scorns!

For which we lose our heads to gild his horns.

PATROCLUS.

The first was Menelaus' kiss; this, mine:

Patroclus kisses you.

MENELAUS.

O, this is trim!

PATROCLUS.

Paris and I kiss evermore for him.

MENELAUS.

I'll have my kiss, sir. Lady, by your leave.

CRESSIDA.

In kissing, do you render or receive?

PATROCLUS.

Both take and give.

CRESSIDA.

I'll make my match to live,

The kiss you take is better than you give;

Therefore no kiss.

MENELAUS.

I'll give you boot; I'll give you three for one.

CRESSIDA.

You are an odd man; give even or give none.

MENELAUS.

An odd man, lady! Every man is odd.

CRESSIDA.

No, Paris is not; for you know 'tis true

That you are odd, and he is even with you.

MENELAUS.

You fillip me o' th'head.

CRESSIDA.

No, I'll be sworn.

ULYSSES.

It were no match, your nail against his horn.

May I, sweet lady, beg a kiss of you?

CRESSIDA.

You may.

ULYSSES.

I do desire it.

CRESSIDA.

Why, beg then.

ULYSSES.

Why then, for Venus' sake give me a kiss

When Helen is a maid again, and his.

CRESSIDA.

I am your debtor; claim it when 'tis due.

ULYSSES.

Never's my day, and then a kiss of you.

DIOMEDES.

Lady, a word. I'll bring you to your father.

[Exit with Cressida.]

NESTOR.

A woman of quick sense.

ULYSSES.

Fie, fie upon her!

There's language in her eye, her cheek, her lip,

Nay, her foot speaks; her wanton spirits look out

At every joint and motive of her body.

O! these encounterers so glib of tongue

That give a coasting welcome ere it comes,

And wide unclasp the tables of their thoughts

To every tickling reader! Set them down

For sluttish spoils of opportunity,

And daughters of the game.

[Trumpet within.]

ALL.

The Trojans' trumpet.

AGAMEMNON.

Yonder comes the troop.

Enter Hector, armed; Aeneas, Troilus, Paris, Deiphobus and other Trojans, with attendants.

AENEAS.

Hail, all you state of Greece! What shall be done

To him that victory commands? Or do you purpose

A victor shall be known? Will you the knights

Shall to the edge of all extremity

Pursue each other, or shall be divided

By any voice or order of the field?

Hector bade ask.

AGAMEMNON.

Which way would Hector have it?

AENEAS.

He cares not; he'll obey conditions.

AGAMEMNON.

'Tis done like Hector.

ACHILLES.

But securely done,

A little proudly, and great deal misprising

The knight oppos'd.

AENEAS.

If not Achilles, sir,

What is your name?

ACHILLES.

If not Achilles, nothing.

AENEAS.

Therefore Achilles. But whate'er, know this:

In the extremity of great and little

Valour and pride excel themselves in Hector;

The one almost as infinite as all,

The other blank as nothing. Weigh him well,

And that which looks like pride is courtesy.

This Ajax is half made of Hector's blood;

In love whereof half Hector stays at home;

Half heart, half hand, half Hector comes to seek

This blended knight, half Trojan and half Greek.

ACHILLES.

A maiden battle then? O! I perceive you.

Re-enter Diomedes.

AGAMEMNON.

Here is Sir Diomed. Go, gentle knight,

Stand by our Ajax. As you and Lord Aeneas

Consent upon the order of their fight,

So be it; either to the uttermost,
Or else a breath. The combatants being kin
Half stints their strife before their strokes begin.

Ajax and Hector enter the lists.

ULYSSES.

They are oppos'd already.

AGAMEMNON.

What Trojan is that same that looks so heavy?

ULYSSES.

The youngest son of Priam, a true knight;
Not yet mature, yet matchless; firm of word;
Speaking in deeds and deedless in his tongue;
Not soon provok'd, nor being provok'd soon calm'd;
His heart and hand both open and both free;
For what he has he gives, what thinks he shows,
Yet gives he not till judgement guide his bounty,
Nor dignifies an impure thought with breath;
Manly as Hector, but more dangerous;
For Hector in his blaze of wrath subscribes
To tender objects, but he in heat of action
Is more vindicative than jealous love.
They call him Troilus, and on him erect
A second hope as fairly built as Hector.

Thus says Aeneas, one that knows the youth

Even to his inches, and, with private soul,

Did in great Ilion thus translate him to me.

[Alarum. Hector and Ajax fight.]

AGAMEMNON.

They are in action.

NESTOR.

Now, Ajax, hold thine own!

TROILUS.

Hector, thou sleep'st; awake thee!

AGAMEMNON.

His blows are well dispos'd. There, Ajax!

[Trumpets cease.]

DIOMEDES.

You must no more.

AENEAS.

Princes, enough, so please you.

AJAX.

I am not warm yet; let us fight again.

DIOMEDES.

As Hector pleases.

HECTOR.

Why, then will I no more.

Thou art, great lord, my father's sister's son,

A cousin-german to great Priam's seed;
The obligation of our blood forbids
A gory emulation 'twixt us twain:
Were thy commixtion Greek and Trojan so
That thou could'st say 'This hand is Grecian all,
And this is Trojan; the sinews of this leg
All Greek, and this all Troy; my mother's blood
Runs on the dexter cheek, and this sinister
Bounds in my father's; by Jove multipotent,
Thou shouldst not bear from me a Greekish member
Wherein my sword had not impressure made
Of our rank feud; but the just gods gainsay
That any drop thou borrow'dst from thy mother,
My sacred aunt, should by my mortal sword
Be drained! Let me embrace thee, Ajax.
By him that thunders, thou hast lusty arms;
Hector would have them fall upon him thus.
Cousin, all honour to thee!

AJAX.

I thank thee, Hector.
Thou art too gentle and too free a man.
I came to kill thee, cousin, and bear hence
A great addition earned in thy death.

HECTOR.

Not Neoptolemus so mirable,

On whose bright crest Fame with her loud'st Oyes

Cries 'This is he!' could promise to himself

A thought of added honour torn from Hector.

AENEAS.

There is expectance here from both the sides

What further you will do.

HECTOR.

We'll answer it:

The issue is embracement. Ajax, farewell.

AJAX.

If I might in entreaties find success,

As seld' I have the chance, I would desire

My famous cousin to our Grecian tents.

DIOMEDES.

'Tis Agamemnon's wish; and great Achilles

Doth long to see unarm'd the valiant Hector.

HECTOR.

Aeneas, call my brother Troilus to me,

And signify this loving interview

To the expecters of our Trojan part;

Desire them home. Give me thy hand, my cousin;

I will go eat with thee, and see your knights.

Agamemnon and the rest of the Greeks come forward.

AJAX.

Great Agamemnon comes to meet us here.

HECTOR.

The worthiest of them tell me name by name;
But for Achilles, my own searching eyes
Shall find him by his large and portly size.

AGAMEMNON.

Worthy all arms! as welcome as to one
That would be rid of such an enemy.
But that's no welcome. Understand more clear,
What's past and what's to come is strew'd with husks
And formless ruin of oblivion;
But in this extant moment, faith and troth,
Strain'd purely from all hollow bias-drawing,
Bids thee with most divine integrity,
From heart of very heart, great Hector, welcome.

HECTOR.

I thank thee, most imperious Agamemnon.

AGAMEMNON.

[To Troilus.] My well-fam'd lord of Troy, no less to you.

MENELAUS.

Let me confirm my princely brother's greeting.

You brace of warlike brothers, welcome hither.

HECTOR.

Who must we answer?

AENEAS.

The noble Menelaus.

HECTOR.

O you, my lord? By Mars his gauntlet, thanks!

Mock not that I affect the untraded oath;

Your quondam wife swears still by Venus' glove.

She's well, but bade me not commend her to you.

MENELAUS.

Name her not now, sir; she's a deadly theme.

HECTOR.

O, pardon; I offend.

NESTOR.

I have, thou gallant Trojan, seen thee oft,

Labouring for destiny, make cruel way

Through ranks of Greekish youth; and I have seen thee,

As hot as Perseus, spur thy Phrygian steed,

Despising many forfeits and subduements,

When thou hast hung thy advanced sword i' th'air,

Not letting it decline on the declined;

That I have said to some my standers-by

'Lo, Jupiter is yonder, dealing life!'

And I have seen thee pause and take thy breath,

When that a ring of Greeks have shrap'd thee in,

Like an Olympian wrestling. This have I seen;

But this thy countenance, still lock'd in steel,

I never saw till now. I knew thy grandsire,

And once fought with him. He was a soldier good,

But, by great Mars, the captain of us all,

Never like thee. O, let an old man embrace thee;

And, worthy warrior, welcome to our tents.

AENEAS.

'Tis the old Nestor.

HECTOR.

Let me embrace thee, good old chronicle,

That hast so long walk'd hand in hand with time.

Most reverend Nestor, I am glad to clasp thee.

NESTOR.

I would my arms could match thee in contention

As they contend with thee in courtesy.

HECTOR.

I would they could.

NESTOR.

Ha!

By this white beard, I'd fight with thee tomorrow.
Well, welcome, welcome! I have seen the time.

ULYSSES.

I wonder now how yonder city stands,
When we have here her base and pillar by us.

HECTOR.

I know your favour, Lord Ulysses, well.
Ah, sir, there's many a Greek and Trojan dead,
Since first I saw yourself and Diomed
In Ilion on your Greekish embassy.

ULYSSES.

Sir, I foretold you then what would ensue.
My prophecy is but half his journey yet;
For yonder walls, that pertly front your town,
Yon towers, whose wanton tops do buss the clouds,
Must kiss their own feet.

HECTOR.

I must not believe you.
There they stand yet; and modestly I think
The fall of every Phrygian stone will cost
A drop of Grecian blood. The end crowns all;
And that old common arbitrator, Time,
Will one day end it.

ULYSSES.

So to him we leave it.

Most gentle and most valiant Hector, welcome.

After the General, I beseech you next

To feast with me and see me at my tent.

ACHILLES.

I shall forestall thee, Lord Ulysses, thou!

Now, Hector, I have fed mine eyes on thee;

I have with exact view perus'd thee, Hector,

And quoted joint by joint.

HECTOR.

Is this Achilles?

ACHILLES.

I am Achilles.

HECTOR.

Stand fair, I pray thee; let me look on thee.

ACHILLES.

Behold thy fill.

HECTOR.

Nay, I have done already.

ACHILLES.

Thou art too brief. I will the second time,

As I would buy thee, view thee limb by limb.

HECTOR.

O, like a book of sport thou'lt read me o'er;

But there's more in me than thou understand'st.

Why dost thou so oppress me with thine eye?

ACHILLES.

Tell me, you heavens, in which part of his body

Shall I destroy him? Whether there, or there, or there?

That I may give the local wound a name,

And make distinct the very breach whereout

Hector's great spirit flew. Answer me, heavens.

HECTOR.

It would discredit the blest gods, proud man,

To answer such a question. Stand again.

Think'st thou to catch my life so pleasantly

As to prenominate in nice conjecture

Where thou wilt hit me dead?

ACHILLES.

I tell thee yea.

HECTOR.

Wert thou an oracle to tell me so,

I'd not believe thee. Henceforth guard thee well;

For I'll not kill thee there, nor there, nor there;

But, by the forge that stithied Mars his helm,

I'll kill thee everywhere, yea, o'er and o'er.

You wisest Grecians, pardon me this brag.

His insolence draws folly from my lips;

But I'll endeavour deeds to match these words,

Or may I never—

AJAX.

Do not chafe thee, cousin;

And you, Achilles, let these threats alone

Till accident or purpose bring you to't.

You may have every day enough of Hector,

If you have stomach. The general state, I fear,

Can scarce entreat you to be odd with him.

HECTOR.

I pray you let us see you in the field;

We have had pelting wars since you refus'd

The Grecians' cause.

ACHILLES.

Dost thou entreat me, Hector?

Tomorrow do I meet thee, fell as death;

Tonight all friends.

HECTOR.

Thy hand upon that match.

AGAMEMNON.

First, all you peers of Greece, go to my tent;
There in the full convive we; afterwards,
As Hector's leisure and your bounties shall
Concur together, severally entreat him.
Beat loud the tambourines, let the trumpets blow,
That this great soldier may his welcome know.

[Exeunt all but Troilus and Ulysses.]

TROILUS.

My Lord Ulysses, tell me, I beseech you,
In what place of the field doth Calchas keep?

ULYSSES.

At Menelaus' tent, most princely Troilus.
There Diomed doth feast with him tonight,
Who neither looks upon the heaven nor earth,
But gives all gaze and bent of amorous view
On the fair Cressid.

TROILUS.

Shall I, sweet lord, be bound to you so much,
After we part from Agamemnon's tent,
To bring me thither?

ULYSSES.

You shall command me, sir.
As gentle tell me of what honour was
This Cressida in Troy? Had she no lover there

That wails her absence?

TROILUS.

O, sir, to such as boasting show their scars

A mock is due. Will you walk on, my lord?

She was belov'd, she lov'd; she is, and doth;

But still sweet love is food for fortune's tooth.

[Exeunt.]

ACT V

SCENE I. The Grecian camp. Before the tent of ACHILLES.

Enter Achilles and Patroclus.

ACHILLES.

I'll heat his blood with Greekish wine tonight,

Which with my scimitar I'll cool tomorrow.

Patroclus, let us feast him to the height.

PATROCLUS.

Here comes Thersites.

Enter Thersites.

ACHILLES.

How now, thou core of envy!

Thou crusty batch of nature, what's the news?

THERSITES.

Why, thou picture of what thou seemest, and idol of idiot worshippers, here's a letter for thee.

ACHILLES.

From whence, fragment?

THERSITES.

Why, thou full dish of fool, from Troy.

PATROCLUS.

Who keeps the tent now?

THERSITES.

The surgeon's box or the patient's wound.

PATROCLUS.

Well said, adversity! And what needs these tricks?

THERSITES.

Prithee, be silent, boy; I profit not by thy talk; thou art said to be Achilles' male varlet.

PATROCLUS.

Male varlet, you rogue! What's that?

THERSITES.

Why, his masculine whore. Now, the rotten diseases of the south, the guts-griping ruptures, catarrhs, loads o' gravel in the back, lethargies, cold palsies, raw eyes, dirt-rotten livers, wheezing lungs, bladders full of imposthume, sciaticas, lime-kilns i' th' palm, incurable bone-ache, and the rivelled fee-simple of the tetter, take and take again such preposterous discoveries!

PATROCLUS.

Why, thou damnable box of envy, thou, what meanest thou to curse thus?

THERSITES.

Do I curse thee?

PATROCLUS.

Why, no, you ruinous butt; you whoreson indistinguishable cur, no.

THERSITES.

No! Why art thou, then, exasperate, thou idle immaterial skein of sleave silk, thou green sarcenet flap for a sore eye, thou tassel of a prodigal's purse, thou? Ah, how the poor world is pestered with such water-flies, diminutives of nature!

PATROCLUS.

Out, gall!

THERSITES.

Finch egg!

ACHILLES.

My sweet Patroclus, I am thwarted quite

From my great purpose in tomorrow's battle.

Here is a letter from Queen Hecuba,

A token from her daughter, my fair love,

Both taxing me and gaging me to keep

An oath that I have sworn. I will not break it.

Fall Greeks; fail fame; honour or go or stay;

My major vow lies here, this I'll obey.

Come, come, Thersites, help to trim my tent;

This night in banqueting must all be spent.

Away, Patroclus!

[Exit with Patroclus.]

THERSITES.

With too much blood and too little brain these two may run mad; but, if with too much brain and too little blood they do, I'll be a curer of madmen. Here's Agamemnon, an honest fellow enough, and one that loves quails, but he has not so much brain as ear-wax; and the goodly transformation of Jupiter there, his brother, the bull, the primitive statue and oblique memorial of cuckolds, a thrifty shoeing-horn in a chain at his brother's leg, to what form but that he is, should wit larded with malice, and malice forced with wit, turn him to? To an ass, were nothing: he is both ass and ox. To an ox, were nothing: he is both ox and ass. To be a dog, a mule, a cat, a fitchook, a toad, a lizard, an owl, a puttock, or a herring without a roe, I would not care; but to be Menelaus, I would conspire against destiny. Ask me not what I would be, if I were not Thersites; for I care not to be the louse of a lazar, so I were not Menelaus. Hey-day! sprites and fires!

Enter Hector, Troilus, Ajax, Agamemnon, Ulysses, Nestor, Menelaus and Diomedes with lights.

AGAMEMNON.

We go wrong, we go wrong.

AJAX.

No, yonder 'tis;

There, where we see the lights.

HECTOR.

I trouble you.

AJAX.

No, not a whit.

ULYSSES.

Here comes himself to guide you.

Re-enter Achilles.

ACHILLES.

Welcome, brave Hector; welcome, Princes all.

AGAMEMNON.

So now, fair Prince of Troy, I bid good night;

Ajax commands the guard to tend on you.

HECTOR.

Thanks, and good night to the Greeks' general.

MENELAUS.

Good night, my lord.

HECTOR.

Good night, sweet Lord Menelaus.

THERSITES.

Sweet draught! 'Sweet' quoth a'!

Sweet sink, sweet sewer!

ACHILLES.

Good night and welcome, both at once, to those

That go or tarry.

AGAMEMNON.

Good night.

[Exeunt Agamemnon and Menelaus.]

ACHILLES.

Old Nestor tarries; and you too, Diomed,

Keep Hector company an hour or two.

DIOMEDES.

I cannot, lord; I have important business,

The tide whereof is now. Good night, great Hector.

HECTOR.

Give me your hand.

ULYSSES.

[Aside to Troilus.] Follow his torch; he goes to

Calchas' tent; I'll keep you company.

TROILUS.

Sweet sir, you honour me.

HECTOR.

And so, good night.

[Exit Diomedes, Ulysses and Troilus following.]

ACHILLES.

Come, come, enter my tent.

[Exeunt all but Thersites.]

THERSITES.

That same Diomed's a false-hearted rogue, a most unjust knave; I will no more trust him when he leers than I will a serpent when he hisses. He will spend his mouth and promise, like Brabbler the hound; but when he performs, astronomers foretell it: it is prodigious, there will come some change; the sun borrows of the moon when Diomed keeps his word. I will rather leave to see Hector than not to dog him. They say he keeps a Trojan drab, and uses the traitor Calchas' tent. I'll after. Nothing but lechery! All incontinent varlets!

[Exit.]

SCENE II. The Grecian camp. Before CALCHAS' tent.

Enter Diomedes.

DIOMEDES.

What, are you up here, ho! Speak.

CALCHAS.

[Within.] Who calls?

DIOMEDES.

Diomed. Calchas, I think. Where's your daughter?

CALCHAS.

[Within.] She comes to you.

Enter Troilus and Ulysses, at a distance; after them Thersites.

ULYSSES.

Stand where the torch may not discover us.

Enter Cressida.

TROILUS.

Cressid comes forth to him.

DIOMEDES.

How now, my charge!

CRESSIDA.

Now, my sweet guardian! Hark, a word with you.

[Whispers.]

TROILUS.

Yea, so familiar?

ULYSSES.

She will sing any man at first sight.

THERSITES.

And any man may sing her, if he can take her cliff; she's noted.

DIOMEDES.

Will you remember?

CRESSIDA.

Remember! Yes.

DIOMEDES.

Nay, but do, then;

And let your mind be coupled with your words.

TROILUS.

What should she remember?

ULYSSES.

List!

CRESSIDA.

Sweet honey Greek, tempt me no more to folly.

THERSITES.

Roguery!

DIOMEDES.

Nay, then—

CRESSIDA.

I'll tell you what—

DIOMEDES.

Fo, fo! come, tell a pin; you are a forsworn.

CRESSIDA.

In faith, I cannot. What would you have me do?

THERSITES.

A juggling trick, to be secretly open.

DIOMEDES.

What did you swear you would bestow on me?

CRESSIDA.

I prithee, do not hold me to mine oath;

Bid me do anything but that, sweet Greek.

DIOMEDES.

Good night.

TROILUS.

Hold, patience!

ULYSSES.

How now, Trojan!

CRESSIDA.

Diomed!

DIOMEDES.

No, no, good night; I'll be your fool no more.

TROILUS.

Thy better must.

CRESSIDA.

Hark! a word in your ear.

TROILUS.

O plague and madness!

ULYSSES.

You are moved, Prince; let us depart, I pray,

Lest your displeasure should enlarge itself

To wrathful terms. This place is dangerous;

The time right deadly; I beseech you, go.

TROILUS.

Behold, I pray you.

ULYSSES.

Nay, good my lord, go off;

You flow to great distraction; come, my lord.

TROILUS.

I pray thee stay.

ULYSSES.

You have not patience; come.

TROILUS.

I pray you, stay; by hell and all hell's torments,

I will not speak a word.

DIOMEDES.

And so, good night.

CRESSIDA.

Nay, but you part in anger.

TROILUS.

Doth that grieve thee? O withered truth!

ULYSSES.

How now, my lord?

TROILUS.

By Jove, I will be patient.

CRESSIDA.

Guardian! Why, Greek!

DIOMEDES.

Fo, fo! adieu! you palter.

CRESSIDA.

In faith, I do not. Come hither once again.

ULYSSES.

You shake, my lord, at something; will you go?

You will break out.

TROILUS.

She strokes his cheek.

ULYSSES.

Come, come.

TROILUS.

Nay, stay; by Jove, I will not speak a word:

There is between my will and all offences

A guard of patience. Stay a little while.

THERSITES.

How the devil Luxury, with his fat rump and potato finger, tickles these together! Fry, lechery, fry!

DIOMEDES.

But will you, then?

CRESSIDA.

In faith, I will, la; never trust me else.

DIOMEDES.

Give me some token for the surety of it.

CRESSIDA.

I'll fetch you one.

[Exit.]

ULYSSES.

You have sworn patience.

TROILUS.

Fear me not, my lord;

I will not be myself, nor have cognition

Of what I feel. I am all patience.

Re-enter Cressida.

THERSITES.

Now the pledge; now, now, now!

CRESSIDA.

Here, Diomed, keep this sleeve.

TROILUS.

O beauty! where is thy faith?

ULYSSES.

My lord!

TROILUS.

I will be patient; outwardly I will.

CRESSIDA.

You look upon that sleeve; behold it well.

He lov'd me—O false wench!—Give't me again.

DIOMEDES.

Whose was't?

CRESSIDA.

It is no matter, now I have't again.

I will not meet with you tomorrow night.

I prithee, Diomed, visit me no more.

THERSITES.

Now she sharpens. Well said, whetstone.

DIOMEDES.

I shall have it.

CRESSIDA.

What, this?

DIOMEDES.

Ay, that.

CRESSIDA.

O all you gods! O pretty, pretty pledge!

Thy master now lies thinking on his bed

Of thee and me, and sighs, and takes my glove,

And gives memorial dainty kisses to it,

As I kiss thee. Nay, do not snatch it from me;

He that takes that doth take my heart withal.

DIOMEDES.

I had your heart before; this follows it.

TROILUS.

I did swear patience.

CRESSIDA.

You shall not have it, Diomed; faith, you shall not;

I'll give you something else.

DIOMEDES.

I will have this. Whose was it?

CRESSIDA.

It is no matter.

DIOMEDES.

Come, tell me whose it was.

CRESSIDA.

'Twas one's that lov'd me better than you will.

But, now you have it, take it.

DIOMEDES.

Whose was it?

CRESSIDA.

By all Diana's waiting women yond,

And by herself, I will not tell you whose.

DIOMEDES.

Tomorrow will I wear it on my helm,

And grieve his spirit that dares not challenge it.

TROILUS.

Wert thou the devil and wor'st it on thy horn,

It should be challeng'd.

CRESSIDA.

Well, well, 'tis done, 'tis past; and yet it is not;

I will not keep my word.

DIOMEDES.

Why, then farewell;

Thou never shalt mock Diomed again.

CRESSIDA.

You shall not go. One cannot speak a word

But it straight starts you.

DIOMEDES.

I do not like this fooling.

THERSITES.

Nor I, by Pluto; but that that likes not you

Pleases me best.

DIOMEDES.

What, shall I come? The hour?

CRESSIDA.

Ay, come; O Jove! Do come. I shall be plagu'd.

DIOMEDES.

Farewell till then.

CRESSIDA.

Good night. I prithee come.

[Exit Diomedes.]

Troilus, farewell! One eye yet looks on thee;

But with my heart the other eye doth see.

Ah, poor our sex! this fault in us I find,

The error of our eye directs our mind.

What error leads must err; O, then conclude,

Minds sway'd by eyes are full of turpitude.

[Exit.]

THERSITES.

A proof of strength she could not publish more,

Unless she said 'My mind is now turn'd whore.'

ULYSSES.

All's done, my lord.

TROILUS.

It is.

ULYSSES.

Why stay we, then?

TROILUS.

To make a recordation to my soul

Of every syllable that here was spoke.

But if I tell how these two did co-act,

Shall I not lie in publishing a truth?

Sith yet there is a credence in my heart,

An esperance so obstinately strong,

That doth invert th'attest of eyes and ears;

As if those organs had deceptious functions

Created only to calumniate.

Was Cressid here?

ULYSSES.

I cannot conjure, Trojan.

TROILUS.

She was not, sure.

ULYSSES.

Most sure she was.

TROILUS.

Why, my negation hath no taste of madness.

ULYSSES.

Nor mine, my lord. Cressid was here but now.

TROILUS.

Let it not be believ'd for womanhood.

Think, we had mothers; do not give advantage

To stubborn critics, apt, without a theme,

For depravation, to square the general sex

By Cressid's rule. Rather think this not Cressid.

ULYSSES.

What hath she done, Prince, that can soil our mothers?

TROILUS.

Nothing at all, unless that this were she.

THERSITES.

Will he swagger himself out on's own eyes?

TROILUS.

This she? No; this is Diomed's Cressida.

If beauty have a soul, this is not she;

If souls guide vows, if vows be sanctimonies,

If sanctimony be the god's delight,

If there be rule in unity itself,

This was not she. O madness of discourse,

That cause sets up with and against itself!

Bi-fold authority! where reason can revolt

Without perdition, and loss assume all reason
Without revolt: this is, and is not, Cressid.
Within my soul there doth conduce a fight
Of this strange nature, that a thing inseparate
Divides more wider than the sky and earth;
And yet the spacious breadth of this division
Admits no orifice for a point as subtle
As Ariachne's broken woof to enter.
Instance, O instance! strong as Pluto's gates:
Cressid is mine, tied with the bonds of heaven.
Instance, O instance! strong as heaven itself:
The bonds of heaven are slipp'd, dissolv'd, and loos'd;
And with another knot, five-finger-tied,
The fractions of her faith, orts of her love,
The fragments, scraps, the bits, and greasy relics
Of her o'er-eaten faith, are given to Diomed.

ULYSSES.

May worthy Troilus be half attach'd
With that which here his passion doth express?

TROILUS.

Ay, Greek; and that shall be divulged well
In characters as red as Mars his heart
Inflam'd with Venus. Never did young man fancy

With so eternal and so fix'd a soul.

Hark, Greek: as much as I do Cressid love,

So much by weight hate I her Diomed.

That sleeve is mine that he'll bear on his helm;

Were it a casque compos'd by Vulcan's skill

My sword should bite it. Not the dreadful spout

Which shipmen do the hurricano call,

Constring'd in mass by the almighty sun,

Shall dizzy with more clamour Neptune's ear

In his descent than shall my prompted sword

Falling on Diomed.

THERSITES.

He'll tickle it for his concupy.

TROILUS.

O Cressid! O false Cressid! false, false, false!

Let all untruths stand by thy stained name,

And they'll seem glorious.

ULYSSES.

O, contain yourself;

Your passion draws ears hither.

Enter Aeneas.

AENEAS.

I have been seeking you this hour, my lord.

Hector, by this, is arming him in Troy;

Ajax, your guard, stays to conduct you home.

TROILUS.

Have with you, Prince. My courteous lord, adieu.

Fairwell, revolted fair! and, Diomed,

Stand fast, and wear a castle on thy head.

ULYSSES.

I'll bring you to the gates.

TROILUS.

Accept distracted thanks.

[Exeunt Troilus, Aeneas and Ulysses.]

THERSITES. Would I could meet that rogue Diomed! I would croak like a raven; I would bode, I would bode. Patroclus will give me anything for the intelligence of this whore; the parrot will not do more for an almond than he for a commodious drab. Lechery, lechery! Still wars and lechery! Nothing else holds fashion. A burning devil take them!

[Exit.]

SCENE III. Troy. Before PRIAM'S palace.

Enter Hector and Andromache.

ANDROMACHE.

When was my lord so much ungently temper'd

To stop his ears against admonishment?

Unarm, unarm, and do not fight today.

HECTOR.

You train me to offend you; get you in.

By all the everlasting gods, I'll go.

ANDROMACHE.

My dreams will, sure, prove ominous to the day.

HECTOR.

No more, I say.

Enter Cassandra.

CASSANDRA.

Where is my brother Hector?

ANDROMACHE.

Here, sister, arm'd, and bloody in intent.

Consort with me in loud and dear petition,

Pursue we him on knees; for I have dreamt

Of bloody turbulence, and this whole night

Hath nothing been but shapes and forms of slaughter.

CASSANDRA.

O, 'tis true!

HECTOR.

Ho! bid my trumpet sound.

CASSANDRA.

No notes of sally, for the heavens, sweet brother!

HECTOR.

Be gone, I say. The gods have heard me swear.

CASSANDRA.

The gods are deaf to hot and peevish vows;

They are polluted off'rings, more abhorr'd

Than spotted livers in the sacrifice.

ANDROMACHE.

O, be persuaded! Do not count it holy

To hurt by being just. It is as lawful,

For we would give much, to use violent thefts

And rob in the behalf of charity.

CASSANDRA.

It is the purpose that makes strong the vow;

But vows to every purpose must not hold.

Unarm, sweet Hector.

HECTOR.

Hold you still, I say.

Mine honour keeps the weather of my fate.
Life every man holds dear; but the dear man
Holds honour far more precious dear than life.

Enter Troilus.

How now, young man! Mean'st thou to fight today?

ANDROMACHE.

Cassandra, call my father to persuade.

[Exit Cassandra.]

HECTOR.

No, faith, young Troilus; doff thy harness, youth;
I am today i' th'vein of chivalry.
Let grow thy sinews till their knots be strong,
And tempt not yet the brushes of the war.
Unarm thee, go; and doubt thou not, brave boy,
I'll stand today for thee and me and Troy.

TROILUS.

Brother, you have a vice of mercy in you,
Which better fits a lion than a man.

HECTOR.

What vice is that? Good Troilus, chide me for it.

TROILUS.

When many times the captive Grecian falls,
Even in the fan and wind of your fair sword,
You bid them rise and live.

HECTOR.

O, 'tis fair play!

TROILUS.

Fool's play, by heaven, Hector.

HECTOR.

How now? how now?

TROILUS.

For th' love of all the gods,

Let's leave the hermit Pity with our mother;

And when we have our armours buckled on,

The venom'd vengeance ride upon our swords,

Spur them to ruthful work, rein them from ruth!

HECTOR.

Fie, savage, fie!

TROILUS.

Hector, then 'tis wars.

HECTOR.

Troilus, I would not have you fight today.

TROILUS.

Who should withhold me?

Not fate, obedience, nor the hand of Mars

Beckoning with fiery truncheon my retire;

Not Priamus and Hecuba on knees,

Their eyes o'er-galled with recourse of tears;

Nor you, my brother, with your true sword drawn,

Oppos'd to hinder me, should stop my way,

But by my ruin.

Re-enter Cassandra with Priam.

CASSANDRA.

Lay hold upon him, Priam, hold him fast;

He is thy crutch; now if thou lose thy stay,

Thou on him leaning, and all Troy on thee,

Fall all together.

PRIAM.

Come, Hector, come, go back.

Thy wife hath dreamt; thy mother hath had visions;

Cassandra doth foresee; and I myself

Am like a prophet suddenly enrapt

To tell thee that this day is ominous.

Therefore, come back.

HECTOR.

Aeneas is a-field;

And I do stand engag'd to many Greeks,

Even in the faith of valour, to appear

This morning to them.

PRIAM.

Ay, but thou shalt not go.

HECTOR.

I must not break my faith.

You know me dutiful; therefore, dear sir,

Let me not shame respect; but give me leave

To take that course by your consent and voice

Which you do here forbid me, royal Priam.

CASSANDRA.

O Priam, yield not to him!

ANDROMACHE.

Do not, dear father.

HECTOR.

Andromache, I am offended with you.

Upon the love you bear me, get you in.

[Exit Andromache.]

TROILUS.

This foolish, dreaming, superstitious girl

Makes all these bodements.

CASSANDRA.

O, farewell, dear Hector!

Look how thou diest. Look how thy eye turns pale.

Look how thy wounds do bleed at many vents.

Hark how Troy roars; how Hecuba cries out;

How poor Andromache shrills her dolours forth;

Behold distraction, frenzy, and amazement,

Like witless antics, one another meet,

And all cry, 'Hector! Hector's dead! O Hector!'

TROILUS.

Away, away!

CASSANDRA.

Farewell! yet, soft! Hector, I take my leave.

Thou dost thyself and all our Troy deceive.

[Exit.]

HECTOR.

You are amaz'd, my liege, at her exclaim.

Go in, and cheer the town; we'll forth, and fight,

Do deeds worth praise and tell you them at night.

PRIAM.

Farewell. The gods with safety stand about thee!

[Exeunt severally Priam and Hector. Alarums.]

TROILUS.

They are at it, hark! Proud Diomed, believe,

I come to lose my arm or win my sleeve.

Enter Pandarus.

PANDARUS.

Do you hear, my lord? Do you hear?

TROILUS.

What now?

PANDARUS.

Here's a letter come from yond poor girl.

TROILUS.

Let me read.

PANDARUS.

A whoreson tisick, a whoreson rascally tisick, so troubles me, and the foolish fortune of this girl, and what one thing, what another, that I shall leave you one o' these days; and I have a rheum in mine eyes too, and such an ache in my bones that unless a man were curs'd I cannot tell what to think on't. What says she there?

TROILUS.

Words, words, mere words, no matter from the heart;

Th'effect doth operate another way.

[Tearing the letter.]

Go, wind, to wind, there turn and change together.

My love with words and errors still she feeds,

But edifies another with her deeds.

[Exeunt severally.]

SCENE IV. The plain between Troy and the Grecian camp.

Alarums. Excursions. Enter Thersites.

THERSITES.

Now they are clapper-clawing one another; I'll go look on. That dissembling abominable varlet, Diomed, has got that same scurvy doting foolish young knave's sleeve of Troy there in his helm. I would fain see them meet, that that same young Trojan ass that loves the whore there might send that Greekish whoremasterly villain with the sleeve back to the dissembling luxurious drab of a sleeve-less errand. O' the other side, the policy of those crafty swearing rascals that stale old mouse-eaten dry cheese, Nestor, and that same dog-fox, Ulysses, is not prov'd worth a blackberry. They set me up, in policy, that mongrel cur, Ajax, against that dog of as bad a kind, Achilles; and now is the cur, Ajax prouder than the cur Achilles, and will not arm today; whereupon the Grecians begin to proclaim barbarism, and policy grows into an ill opinion.

Enter Diomedes, Troilus following.

Soft! here comes sleeve, and t'other.

TROILUS.

Fly not; for shouldst thou take the river Styx, I would swim after.

DIOMEDES.

Thou dost miscall retire.

I do not fly; but advantageous care

Withdrew me from the odds of multitude.

Have at thee!

THERSITES.

Hold thy whore, Grecian; now for thy whore,

Trojan! now the sleeve, now the sleeve!

[Exeunt Troilus and Diomedes fighting.]

Enter Hector.

HECTOR.

What art thou, Greek? Art thou for Hector's match?

Art thou of blood and honour?

THERSITES.

No, no I am a rascal; a scurvy railing knave; a very filthy rogue.

HECTOR.

I do believe thee. Live.

[Exit.]

THERSITES.

God-a-mercy, that thou wilt believe me; but a plague break thy neck for frighting me! What's become of the wenching rogues? I think they have swallowed one another. I would laugh at that miracle. Yet, in a sort, lechery eats itself. I'll seek them.

[Exit.]

SCENE V. Another part of the plain.

Enter Diomedes and a Servant.

DIOMEDES.

Go, go, my servant, take thou Troilus' horse;

Present the fair steed to my lady Cressid.

Fellow, commend my service to her beauty;

Tell her I have chastis'd the amorous Trojan,

And am her knight by proof.

SERVANT.

I go, my lord.

[Exit.]

Enter Agamemnon.

AGAMEMNON.

Renew, renew! The fierce Polydamas

Hath beat down Menon; bastard Margarelon

Hath Doreus prisoner,

And stands colossus-wise, waving his beam,

Upon the pashed corses of the kings

Epistrophus and Cedius. Polixenes is slain;

Amphimacus and Thoas deadly hurt;

Patroclus ta'en, or slain; and Palamedes

Sore hurt and bruis'd. The dreadful Sagittary

Appals our numbers. Haste we, Diomed,

To reinforcement, or we perish all.

Enter Nestor.

NESTOR.

Go, bear Patroclus' body to Achilles,

And bid the snail-pac'd Ajax arm for shame.

There is a thousand Hectors in the field;

Now here he fights on Galathe his horse,

And there lacks work; anon he's there afoot,

And there they fly or die, like scaled sculls

Before the belching whale; then is he yonder,

And there the strawy Greeks, ripe for his edge,

Fall down before him like the mower's swath.

Here, there, and everywhere, he leaves and takes;

Dexterity so obeying appetite

That what he will he does, and does so much

That proof is call'd impossibility.

Enter Ulysses.

ULYSSES.

O, courage, courage, courage, Princes! Great Achilles

Is arming, weeping, cursing, vowing vengeance.

Patroclus' wounds have rous'd his drowsy blood,

Together with his mangled Myrmidons,

That noseless, handless, hack'd and chipp'd, come to him,

Crying on Hector. Ajax hath lost a friend
And foams at mouth, and he is arm'd and at it,
Roaring for Troilus; who hath done today
Mad and fantastic execution,
Engaging and redeeming of himself
With such a careless force and forceless care
As if that lust, in very spite of cunning,
Bade him win all.

Enter Ajax.

AJAX.

Troilus! thou coward Troilus!

[Exit.]

DIOMEDES.

Ay, there, there.

NESTOR.

So, so, we draw together.

[Exit.]

Enter Achilles.

ACHILLES.

Where is this Hector?
Come, come, thou boy-queller, show thy face;
Know what it is to meet Achilles angry.
Hector! where's Hector? I will none but Hector.

[Exeunt.]

SCENE VI. Another part of the plain.

Enter Ajax.

AJAX.

Troilus, thou coward Troilus, show thy head.

Enter Diomedes.

DIOMEDES.

Troilus, I say! Where's Troilus?

AJAX.

What wouldst thou?

DIOMEDES.

I would correct him.

AJAX.

Were I the general, thou shouldst have my office

Ere that correction. Troilus, I say! What, Troilus!

Enter Troilus.

TROILUS.

O traitor Diomed! Turn thy false face, thou traitor,

And pay thy life thou owest me for my horse.

DIOMEDES.

Ha! art thou there?

AJAX.

I'll fight with him alone. Stand, Diomed.

DIOMEDES.

He is my prize. I will not look upon.

TROILUS.

Come, both, you cogging Greeks; have at you both!

[Exeunt fighting.]

Enter Hector.

HECTOR.

Yea, Troilus? O, well fought, my youngest brother!

Enter Achilles.

ACHILLES.

Now do I see thee. Ha! have at thee, Hector!

HECTOR.

Pause, if thou wilt.

ACHILLES.

I do disdain thy courtesy, proud Trojan.

Be happy that my arms are out of use;

My rest and negligence befriend thee now,

But thou anon shalt hear of me again;

Till when, go seek thy fortune.

[Exit.]

HECTOR.

Fare thee well.

I would have been much more a fresher man,

Had I expected thee.

Re-enter Troilus.

How now, my brother!

TROILUS.

Ajax hath ta'en Aeneas. Shall it be?
No, by the flame of yonder glorious heaven,
He shall not carry him; I'll be ta'en too,
Or bring him off. Fate, hear me what I say:
I reck not though thou end my life today.

[Exit.]

Enter one in armour.

HECTOR.

Stand, stand, thou Greek; thou art a goodly mark.
No? wilt thou not? I like thy armour well;
I'll frush it and unlock the rivets all
But I'll be master of it. Wilt thou not, beast, abide?
Why then, fly on; I'll hunt thee for thy hide.

[Exeunt.]

SCENE VII. Another part of the plain.

Enter Achilles with Myrmidons.

ACHILLES.

Come here about me, you my Myrmidons;

Mark what I say. Attend me where I wheel;

Strike not a stroke, but keep yourselves in breath;

And when I have the bloody Hector found,

Empale him with your weapons round about;

In fellest manner execute your arms.

Follow me, sirs, and my proceedings eye.

It is decreed Hector the great must die.

[Exeunt.]

Enter Menelaus and Paris, fighting; then Thersites.

THERSITES.

The cuckold and the cuckold-maker are at it. Now, bull! Now, dog! 'Loo, Paris, 'loo! now my double-hen'd Spartan! 'loo, Paris, 'loo! The bull has the game. 'Ware horns, ho!

[Exeunt Paris and Menelaus.]

Enter Margarelon.

MARGARELON.

Turn, slave, and fight.

THERSITES.

What art thou?

MARGARELON.

A bastard son of Priam's.

THERSITES.

I am a bastard too; I love bastards. I am a bastard begot, bastard instructed, bastard in mind, bastard in valour, in everything illegitimate. One bear will not bite another, and wherefore should one bastard? Take heed, the quarrel's most ominous to us: if the son of a whore fight for a whore, he tempts judgement. Farewell, bastard.

[Exit.]

MARGARELON.

The devil take thee, coward!

[Exit.]

SCENE VIII. Another part of the plain.

Enter Hector.

HECTOR.

Most putrified core so fair without,

Thy goodly armour thus hath cost thy life.

Now is my day's work done; I'll take my breath:

Rest, sword; thou hast thy fill of blood and death!

[Disarms.]

Enter Achilles and Myrmidons.

ACHILLES.

Look, Hector, how the sun begins to set,

How ugly night comes breathing at his heels;

Even with the vail and dark'ning of the sun,

To close the day up, Hector's life is done.

HECTOR.

I am unarm'd; forego this vantage, Greek.

ACHILLES.

Strike, fellows, strike; this is the man I seek.

[Hector falls.]

So, Ilion, fall thou next! Now, Troy, sink down;

Here lies thy heart, thy sinews, and thy bone.

On, Myrmidons, and cry you all amain

'Achilles hath the mighty Hector slain.'

[A retreat sounded.]

Hark! a retire upon our Grecian part.

MYRMIDON.

The Trojan trumpets sound the like, my lord.

ACHILLES.

The dragon wing of night o'erspreads the earth

And, stickler-like, the armies separates.

My half-supp'd sword, that frankly would have fed,

Pleas'd with this dainty bait, thus goes to bed.

[Sheathes his sword.]

Come, tie his body to my horse's tail;

Along the field I will the Trojan trail.

[Exeunt.]

SCENE IX. Another part of the plain.

Sound retreat. Shout. Enter Agamemnon, Ajax, Menelaus, Nestor, Diomedes and the rest, marching.

AGAMEMNON.

Hark! hark! what shout is this?

NESTOR.

Peace, drums!

SOLDIERS.

[Within.] Achilles! Achilles! Hector's slain. Achilles!

DIOMEDES.

The bruit is, Hector's slain, and by Achilles.

AJAX.

If it be so, yet bragless let it be;

Great Hector was as good a man as he.

AGAMEMNON.

March patiently along. Let one be sent

To pray Achilles see us at our tent.

If in his death the gods have us befriended;

Great Troy is ours, and our sharp wars are ended.

[Exeunt.]

SCENE X. Another part of the plain.

Enter Aeneas, Paris, Antenor and Deiphobus.

AENEAS.

Stand, ho! yet are we masters of the field.

Never go home; here starve we out the night.

Enter Troilus.

TROILUS.

Hector is slain.

ALL.

Hector! The gods forbid!

TROILUS.

He's dead, and at the murderer's horse's tail,

In beastly sort, dragg'd through the shameful field.

Frown on, you heavens, effect your rage with speed.

Sit, gods, upon your thrones, and smile at Troy.

I say at once let your brief plagues be mercy,

And linger not our sure destructions on.

AENEAS.

My lord, you do discomfort all the host.

TROILUS.

You understand me not that tell me so.

I do not speak of flight, of fear of death,

But dare all imminence that gods and men
Address their dangers in. Hector is gone.
Who shall tell Priam so, or Hecuba?
Let him that will a screech-owl aye be call'd
Go in to Troy, and say there 'Hector's dead.'
There is a word will Priam turn to stone;
Make wells and Niobes of the maids and wives,
Cold statues of the youth; and, in a word,
Scare Troy out of itself. But, march away;
Hector is dead; there is no more to say.
Stay yet. You vile abominable tents,
Thus proudly pight upon our Phrygian plains,
Let Titan rise as early as he dare,
I'll through and through you. And, thou great-siz'd coward,
No space of earth shall sunder our two hates;
I'll haunt thee like a wicked conscience still,
That mouldeth goblins swift as frenzy's thoughts.
Strike a free march to Troy. With comfort go;
Hope of revenge shall hide our inward woe.

Enter Pandarus.

PANDARUS.

But hear you, hear you!

TROILUS.

Hence, broker-lackey. Ignominy and shame

Pursue thy life, and live aye with thy name!

[Exeunt all but Pandarus.]

PANDARUS.

A goodly medicine for my aching bones! O world! world! Thus is the poor agent despis'd! O traitors and bawds, how earnestly are you set a-work, and how ill requited! Why should our endeavour be so lov'd, and the performance so loathed? What verse for it? What instance for it? Let me see—

Full merrily the humble-bee doth sing

Till he hath lost his honey and his sting;

And being once subdu'd in armed trail,

Sweet honey and sweet notes together fail.

Good traders in the flesh, set this in your painted cloths.

As many as be here of Pandar's hall,

Your eyes, half out, weep out at Pandar's fall;

Or, if you cannot weep, yet give some groans,

Though not for me, yet for your aching bones.

Brethren and sisters of the hold-door trade,

Some two months hence my will shall here be made.

It should be now, but that my fear is this,

Some galled goose of Winchester would hiss.

Till then I'll sweat and seek about for eases,

And at that time bequeath you my diseases.

[Exit.]

About Author

Shakespeare produced most of his known works between 1589 and 1613. His early plays were primarily comedies and histories and are regarded as some of the best work produced in these genres. Until about 1608, he wrote mainly tragedies, among them Hamlet, Othello, King Lear, and Macbeth, all considered to be among the finest works in the English language. In the last phase of his life, he wrote tragicomedies (also known as romances) and collaborated with other playwrights.

Many of Shakespeare's plays were published in editions of varying quality and accuracy in his lifetime. However, in 1623, two fellow actors and friends of Shakespeare's, John Heminges and Henry Condell, published a more definitive text known as the First Folio, a posthumous collected edition of Shakespeare's dramatic works that included all but two of his plays. The volume was prefaced with a poem by Ben Jonson, in which Jonson presciently hails Shakespeare in a now-famous quote as "not of an age, but for all time".

Throughout the 20th and 21st centuries, Shakespeare's works have been continually adapted and rediscovered by new movements in scholarship and performance. His plays remain popular and are studied, performed, and reinterpreted through various cultural and political contexts around the world.

Early life

William Shakespeare was the son of John Shakespeare, an alderman and a successful glover (glove-maker) originally from Snitterfield, and Mary Arden, the daughter of an affluent landowning farmer. He was born in Stratford-upon-Avon and baptised there on 26 April 1564. His actual date of birth remains unknown, but is traditionally observed on 23 April, Saint George's Day. This date, which can be traced to a mistake made by an 18th-century scholar, has proved appealing to biographers because Shakespeare died on the same date in 1616. He was the third of eight children, and the eldest surviving son.

Although no attendance records for the period survive, most biographers agree that Shakespeare was probably educated at the King's New School in Stratford, a free school chartered in 1553, about a quarter-mile (400 m) from his home. Grammar schools varied in quality during the Elizabethan era, but grammar school curricula were largely similar: the basic Latin text was standardised by royal decree, and the school would have provided an intensive education in grammar based upon Latin classical authors.

At the age of 18, Shakespeare married 26-year-old Anne Hathaway. The consistory court of the Diocese of Worcester issued a marriage licence on 27 November 1582. The next day, two of Hathaway's neighbours posted bonds guaranteeing that no lawful claims impeded the marriage. The ceremony may have been arranged in some haste since the Worcester chancellor allowed the marriage banns to be read once instead of the usual three times, and six months after the marriage Anne gave birth to a daughter, Susanna, baptised 26 May 1583. Twins, son Hamnet and daughter Judith, followed almost two years later and were baptised 2 February 1585. Hamnet died of unknown causes at the age of 11 and was buried 11 August 1596.

After the birth of the twins, Shakespeare left few historical traces until he is mentioned as part of the London theatre scene in 1592. The exception is the appearance of his name in the "complaints bill" of a law case before the Queen's Bench court at Westminster dated Michaelmas Term 1588 and 9 October 1589. Scholars refer to the years between 1585 and 1592 as Shakespeare's "lost years". Biographers attempting to account for this period have reported many apocryphal stories. Nicholas Rowe, Shakespeare's first biographer, recounted a Stratford legend that Shakespeare fled the town for London to escape prosecution for deer poaching in the estate of local squire Thomas Lucy. Shakespeare is also supposed to have taken his revenge on Lucy by writing a scurrilous ballad about him. Another 18th-century story has Shakespeare starting his theatrical career minding the horses of theatre patrons in London. John Aubrey reported that Shakespeare had been a country schoolmaster. Some 20th-century scholars have suggested that Shakespeare may have been employed as a schoolmaster by Alexander

Hoghton of Lancashire, a Catholic landowner who named a certain "William Shakeshafte" in his will. Little evidence substantiates such stories other than hearsay collected after his death, and Shakeshafte was a common name in the Lancashire area.

London and theatrical career

It is not known definitively when Shakespeare began writing, but contemporary allusions and records of performances show that several of his plays were on the London stage by 1592. By then, he was sufficiently known in London to be attacked in print by the playwright Robert Greene in his Groats-Worth of Wit:

... there is an upstart Crow, beautified with our feathers, that with his Tiger's heart wrapped in a Player's hide, supposes he is as well able to bombast out a blank verse as the best of you: and being an absolute Johannes factotum, is in his own conceit the only Shake-scene in a country.

Scholars differ on the exact meaning of Greene's words, but most agree that Greene was accusing Shakespeare of reaching above his rank in trying to match such university-educated writers as Christopher Marlowe, Thomas Nashe, and Greene himself (the so-called "University Wits"). The italicised phrase parodying the line "Oh, tiger's heart wrapped in a woman's hide" from Shakespeare's Henry VI, Part 3, along with the pun "Shake-scene", clearly identify Shakespeare as Greene's target. As used here, Johannes Factotum ("Jack of all trades") refers to a second-rate tinkerer with the work of others, rather than the more common "universal genius".

Greene's attack is the earliest surviving mention of Shakespeare's work in the theatre. Biographers suggest that his career may have begun any time from the mid-1580s to just before Greene's remarks. After 1594, Shakespeare's plays were performed only by the Lord Chamberlain's Men, a company owned by a group of players, including Shakespeare, that soon became the leading playing company in London. After the death of Queen Elizabeth in 1603, the company was awarded a royal patent by the new King James I, and changed its name to the King's Men.

"All the world's a stage,
and all the men and women merely players:
they have their exits and their entrances;
and one man in his time plays many parts ..."
—As You Like It, Act II, Scene 7, 139–142

In 1599, a partnership of members of the company built their own theatre on the south bank of the River Thames, which they named the Globe. In 1608, the partnership also took over the Blackfriars indoor theatre. Extant records of Shakespeare's property purchases and investments indicate that his association with the company made him a wealthy man, and in 1597, he bought the second-largest house in Stratford, New Place, and in 1605, invested in a share of the parish tithes in Stratford.

Some of Shakespeare's plays were published in quarto editions, beginning in 1594, and by 1598, his name had become a selling point and began to appear on the title pages. Shakespeare continued to act in his own and other plays after his success as a playwright. The 1616 edition of Ben Jonson's Works names him on the cast lists for Every Man in His Humour (1598) and Sejanus His Fall (1603). The absence of his name from the 1605 cast list for Jonson's Volpone is taken by some scholars as a sign that his acting career was nearing its end. The First Folio of 1623, however, lists Shakespeare as one of "the Principal Actors in all these Plays", some of which were first staged after Volpone, although we cannot know for certain which roles he played. In 1610, John Davies of Hereford wrote that "good Will" played "kingly" roles. In 1709, Rowe passed down a tradition that Shakespeare played the ghost of Hamlet's father. Later traditions maintain that he also played Adam in As You Like It, and the Chorus in Henry V, though scholars doubt the sources of that information.

Throughout his career, Shakespeare divided his time between London and Stratford. In 1596, the year before he bought New Place as his family home in Stratford, Shakespeare was living in the parish of St. Helen's, Bishopsgate, north of the River Thames. He moved across the river to Southwark by 1599, the same year his company constructed the Globe Theatre there. By 1604, he had moved north of the river again, to an area north of St Paul's Cathedral with many fine houses. There, he rented rooms from a French Huguenot named Christopher Mountjoy, a maker of ladies' wigs and other headgear.

Later years and death

Rowe was the first biographer to record the tradition, repeated by Johnson, that Shakespeare retired to Stratford "some years before his death". He was still working as an actor in London in 1608; in an answer to the sharers' petition in 1635, Cuthbert Burbage stated that after purchasing the lease of the Blackfriars Theatre in 1608 from Henry Evans, the King's Men "placed men players" there, "which were Heminges, Condell, Shakespeare, etc.". However, it is perhaps relevant that the bubonic plague raged in London throughout 1609. The London public playhouses were repeatedly closed during extended outbreaks of the plague (a total of over 60 months closure between May 1603 and February 1610), which meant there was often no acting work. Retirement from all work was uncommon at that time. Shakespeare continued to visit London during the years 1611–1614. In 1612, he was called as a witness in Bellott v. Mountjoy, a court case concerning the marriage settlement of Mountjoy's daughter, Mary. In March 1613, he bought a gatehouse in the former Blackfriars priory; and from November 1614, he was in London for several weeks with his son-in-law, John Hall. After 1610, Shakespeare wrote fewer plays, and none are attributed to him after 1613. His last three plays were collaborations, probably with John Fletcher, who succeeded him as the house playwright of the King's Men.

Shakespeare died on 23 April 1616, at the age of 52. He died within a month of signing his will, a document which he begins by describing himself as being in "perfect health". No extant contemporary source explains how or why he died. Half a century later, John Ward, the vicar of Stratford, wrote in his notebook: "Shakespeare, Drayton, and Ben Jonson had a merry meeting and, it seems, drank too hard, for Shakespeare died of a fever there contracted", not an impossible scenario since Shakespeare knew Jonson and Drayton. Of the tributes from fellow authors, one refers to his relatively sudden death: "We wondered, Shakespeare, that thou went'st so soon / From the world's stage to the grave's tiring room."

He was survived by his wife and two daughters. Susanna had married a physician, John Hall, in 1607, and Judith had married Thomas Quiney, a vintner, two months before Shakespeare's death. Shakespeare signed his last will and testament on 25 March 1616; the following day, his new son-in-law, Thomas Quiney was found guilty of fathering an illegitimate son by Margaret Wheeler, who had died during childbirth. Thomas was ordered by the church court to do public penance, which would have caused much shame and embarrassment for the Shakespeare family.

Shakespeare bequeathed the bulk of his large estate to his elder daughter Susanna under stipulations that she pass it down intact to "the first son of her body". The Quincys had three children, all of whom died without marrying. The Halls had one child, Elizabeth, who married twice but died without children in 1670, ending Shakespeare's direct line. Shakespeare's will scarcely mentions his wife, Anne, who was probably entitled to one-third of his estate automatically. He did make a point, however, of leaving her "my second best bed", a bequest that has led to much speculation. Some scholars see the bequest as an insult to Anne, whereas others believe that the second-best bed would have been the matrimonial bed and therefore rich in significance.

Shakespeare was buried in the chancel of the Holy Trinity Church two days after his death. The epitaph carved into the stone slab covering his grave includes a curse against moving his bones, which was carefully avoided during restoration of the church in 2008:

Good frend for Iesvs sake forbeare,

To digg the dvst encloased heare.

Bleste be Middle English the.svg man Middle English that.svg spares thes stones,

And cvrst be he Middle English that.svg moves my bones.

(Modern spelling: Good friend, for Jesus' sake forbear, / To dig the dust enclosed here. / Blessed be the man that spares these stones, / And cursed be he that moves my bones.)

Some time before 1623, a funerary monument was erected in his memory on the north wall, with a half-effigy of him in the act of writing. Its plaque compares him to Nestor, Socrates, and Virgil. In 1623, in conjunction with the publication of the First Folio, the Droeshout engraving was published.

Shakespeare has been commemorated in many statues and memorials around the world, including funeral monuments in Southwark Cathedral and Poets' Corner in Westminster Abbey.

Plays

Most playwrights of the period typically collaborated with others at some point, and critics agree that Shakespeare did the same, mostly early and late in his career. Some attributions, such as Titus Andronicus and the early history plays, remain controversial while The Two Noble Kinsmen and the lost Cardenio have well-attested contemporary documentation. Textual evidence also supports the view that several of the plays were revised by other writers after their original composition.

The first recorded works of Shakespeare are Richard III and the three parts of Henry VI, written in the early 1590s during a vogue for historical drama. Shakespeare's plays are difficult to date precisely, however, and studies of the texts suggest that Titus Andronicus, The Comedy of Errors, The Taming of the Shrew, and The Two Gentlemen of Verona may also belong to Shakespeare's earliest period. His first histories, which draw heavily on the 1587 edition of Raphael Holinshed's Chronicles of England, Scotland, and Ireland, dramatise the destructive results of weak or corrupt rule and have been interpreted as a justification for the origins of the Tudor dynasty. The early plays were influenced by the works of other Elizabethan dramatists, especially Thomas Kyd and Christopher Marlowe, by the traditions of medieval drama, and by the plays of Seneca. The Comedy of Errors was also based on classical models, but no source for The Taming of the Shrew has been found, though it is related to a separate play of the same name and may have derived from a folk story. Like The Two Gentlemen of Verona, in which two friends appear to approve of rape, the Shrew's story of the taming of a woman's independent spirit by a man sometimes troubles modern critics, directors, and audiences.

Shakespeare's early classical and Italianate comedies, containing tight double plots and precise comic sequences, give way in the mid-1590s to the romantic atmosphere of his most acclaimed comedies. A Midsummer Night's Dream is a witty mixture of romance, fairy magic, and comic lowlife scenes. Shakespeare's next comedy, the equally romantic Merchant of Venice, contains a portrayal of the vengeful Jewish moneylender Shylock, which reflects Elizabethan views but may appear derogatory to modern audiences. The wit and wordplay of Much Ado About Nothing, the charming rural setting of As You Like It, and the lively merrymaking of Twelfth Night complete Shakespeare's sequence of great comedies. After the lyrical Richard II, written almost entirely in verse, Shakespeare introduced prose comedy into the histories of the late 1590s, Henry IV, parts 1 and 2, and Henry V. His characters become more complex and tender as he switches deftly between comic and serious scenes, prose and poetry, and achieves the narrative variety of his mature work. This period begins and ends with two tragedies: Romeo and Juliet, the famous romantic tragedy of sexually charged adolescence, love, and death; and Julius Caesar—based on Sir Thomas North's 1579 translation of Plutarch's Parallel Lives—which introduced a new kind of drama. According to Shakespearean scholar James Shapiro, in Julius Caesar, "the various strands of politics, character, inwardness, contemporary events, even Shakespeare's own reflections on the act of writing, began to infuse each other".

In the early 17th century, Shakespeare wrote the so-called "problem plays" Measure for Measure, Troilus and Cressida, and All's Well That Ends Well and a number of his best known tragedies. Many critics believe that Shakespeare's greatest tragedies represent the peak of his art. The titular hero of one of Shakespeare's greatest tragedies, Hamlet, has probably been discussed more than any other Shakespearean character, especially for his famous soliloquy which begins "To be or not to be; that is the question". Unlike the introverted Hamlet, whose fatal flaw is hesitation, the heroes of the tragedies that followed, Othello and King Lear, are undone by hasty errors of judgement. The plots of Shakespeare's tragedies often hinge on such fatal errors or flaws, which overturn order and destroy the hero and those he loves. In Othello, the villain Iago stokes Othello's sexual jealousy to the point where he murders the innocent wife who loves him. In King Lear, the old king commits the tragic error of giving up his powers, initiating the events which lead to the torture and blinding of the Earl of Gloucester and the murder of Lear's youngest daughter Cordelia. According to the critic Frank Kermode, "the play-offers neither its good characters nor its audience any relief from its cruelty". In Macbeth, the shortest and most compressed of Shakespeare's tragedies, uncontrollable ambition incites Macbeth and his wife, Lady Macbeth, to murder the rightful king and usurp the throne until their own guilt destroys them in turn. In this play, Shakespeare adds a supernatural element to the tragic structure. His last major tragedies, Antony and Cleopatra and Coriolanus, contain some of Shakespeare's finest poetry and were considered his most successful tragedies by the poet and critic T.S. Eliot.

In his final period, Shakespeare turned to romance or tragicomedy and completed three more major plays: Cymbeline, The Winter's Tale, and The Tempest, as well as the collaboration, Pericles, Prince of Tyre. Less bleak than the tragedies, these four plays are graver in tone than the comedies of the 1590s, but they end with reconciliation and the forgiveness of potentially tragic errors. Some commentators have seen this change in mood as evidence of a more serene view of life on Shakespeare's part, but it may merely reflect the theatrical fashion of the day. Shakespeare collaborated on two further surviving plays, Henry VIII and The Two Noble Kinsmen, probably with John Fletcher.

Performances

It is not clear for which companies Shakespeare wrote his early plays. The title page of the 1594 edition of Titus Andronicus reveals that the play had been acted by three different troupes. After the plagues of 1592–3, Shakespeare's plays were performed by his own company at The Theatre and the Curtain in Shoreditch, north of the Thames. Londoners flocked there to see the first part of Henry IV, Leonard Digges recording, "Let but Falstaff come, Hal, Poins, the rest ... and you scarce shall have a room". When the company found themselves in dispute with their landlord, they pulled The

Theatre down and used the timbers to construct the Globe Theatre, the first playhouse built by actors for actors, on the south bank of the Thames at Southwark. The Globe opened in autumn 1599, with Julius Caesar one of the first plays staged. Most of Shakespeare's greatest post-1599 plays were written for the Globe, including Hamlet, Othello, and King Lear.

After the Lord Chamberlain's Men were renamed the King's Men in 1603, they entered a special relationship with the new King James. Although the performance records are patchy, the King's Men performed seven of Shakespeare's plays at court between 1 November 1604, and 31 October 1605, including two performances of The Merchant of Venice. After 1608, they performed at the indoor Blackfriars Theatre during the winter and the Globe during the summer. The indoor setting, combined with the Jacobean fashion for lavishly staged masques, allowed Shakespeare to introduce more elaborate stage devices. In Cymbeline, for example, Jupiter descends "in thunder and lightning, sitting upon an eagle: he throws a thunderbolt. The ghosts fall on their knees."

The actors in Shakespeare's company included the famous Richard Burbage, William Kempe, Henry Condell and John Heminges. Burbage played the leading role in the first performances of many of Shakespeare's plays, including Richard III, Hamlet, Othello, and King Lear. The popular comic actor Will Kempe played the servant Peter in Romeo and Juliet and Dogberry in Much Ado About Nothing, among other characters. He was replaced around 1600 by Robert Armin, who played roles such as Touchstone in As You Like It and the fool in King Lear. In 1613, Sir Henry Wotton recorded that Henry VIII "was set forth with many extraordinary circumstances of pomp and ceremony". On 29 June, however, a cannon set fire to the thatch of the Globe and burned the theatre to the ground, an event which pinpoints the date of a Shakespeare play with rare precision.

Textual sources

In 1623, John Heminges and Henry Condell, two of Shakespeare's friends from the King's Men, published the First Folio, a collected edition of Shakespeare's plays. It contained 36 texts, including 18 printed for the first time. Many of the plays had already appeared in quarto versions—flimsy books made from sheets of paper folded twice to make four leaves. No evidence suggests that Shakespeare approved these editions, which the First Folio describes as "stol'n and surreptitious copies". Nor did Shakespeare plan or expect his works to survive in any form at all; those works likely would have faded into oblivion but for his friends' spontaneous idea, after his death, to create and publish the First Folio.

Alfred Pollard termed some of the pre-1623 versions as "bad quartos" because of their adapted, paraphrased or garbled texts, which may in places have been reconstructed from memory. Where several versions of a play survive, each differs from the other. The differences may stem from copying or printing errors, from notes by actors or audience members, or from Shakespeare's own papers. In some cases, for example, Hamlet, Troilus and Cressida, and Othello, Shakespeare could have revised the texts between the quarto and folio editions. In the case of King Lear, however, while most modern editions do conflate them, the 1623 folio version is so different from the 1608 quarto that the Oxford Shakespeare prints them both, arguing that they cannot be conflated without confusion.

Influence from neighbours in London

Ten years of research by Geoffrey Marsh (museum director) of the Victoria and Albert Museum in London may have shown that Shakespeare got many of the ideas and information for his plays, from his neighbours that he lived near in London in the late 1590s.

Geoffrey Marsh found the site of Shakespeare's house in St Helen's Church, Bishopsgate parish, at the corner of St.Helen's churchyard and Bishopsgate Street, north of the churchyard, from the records of the Leathersellers Company. Many wealthy and notable people (including Sir John Spencer and Dr. Edward Jorden and Dr. Peter Turner), with connections across Europe, lived near Shakespeare.

Poems

In 1593 and 1594, when the theatres were closed because of plague,

Shakespeare published two narrative poems on sexual themes, Venus and Adonis and The Rape of Lucrece. He dedicated them to Henry Wriothesley, Earl of Southampton. In Venus and Adonis, an innocent Adonis rejects the sexual advances of Venus; while in The Rape of Lucrece, the virtuous wife Lucrece is raped by the lustful Tarquin. Influenced by Ovid's Metamorphoses, the poems show the guilt and moral confusion that result from uncontrolled lust. Both proved popular and were often reprinted during Shakespeare's lifetime. A third narrative poem, A Lover's Complaint, in which a young woman laments her seduction by a persuasive suitor, was printed in the first edition of the Sonnets in 1609. Most scholars now accept that Shakespeare wrote A Lover's Complaint. Critics consider that its fine qualities are marred by leaden effects. The Phoenix and the Turtle, printed in Robert Chester's 1601 Love's Martyr, mourns the deaths of the legendary phoenix and his lover, the faithful turtle dove. In 1599, two early drafts of sonnets 138 and 144 appeared in The Passionate Pilgrim, published under Shakespeare's name but without his permission.

Sonnets

Published in 1609, the Sonnets were the last of Shakespeare's non-dramatic works to be printed. Scholars are not certain when each of the 154 sonnets was composed, but evidence suggests that Shakespeare wrote sonnets throughout his career for a private readership. Even before the two unauthorised sonnets appeared in The Passionate Pilgrim in 1599, Francis Meres had referred in 1598 to Shakespeare's "sugred Sonnets among his private friends". Few analysts believe that the published collection follows Shakespeare's intended sequence. He seems to have planned two contrasting series: one about uncontrollable lust for a married woman of dark complexion (the "dark lady"), and one about conflicted love for a fair young man (the "fair youth"). It remains unclear if these figures represent real individuals, or if the authorial "I" who addresses them represents Shakespeare himself, though Wordsworth believed that with the sonnets "Shakespeare unlocked his heart".

"Shall I compare thee to a summer's day?

Thou art more lovely and more temperate ..."

—Lines from Shakespeare's Sonnet 18.

The 1609 edition was dedicated to a "Mr. W.H.", credited as "the only begetter" of the poems. It is not known whether this was written by Shakespeare himself or by the publisher, Thomas Thorpe, whose initials appear at the foot of the dedication page; nor is it known who Mr. W.H. was, despite numerous theories, or whether Shakespeare even authorised the publication. Critics praise the Sonnets as a profound meditation on the nature of love, sexual passion, procreation, death, and time.

Style

Shakespeare's first plays were written in the conventional style of the day. He wrote them in a stylised language that does not always spring naturally from the needs of the characters or the drama. The poetry depends on extended, sometimes elaborate metaphors and conceits, and the language is often rhetorical—written for actors to declaim rather than speak. The grand speeches in Titus Andronicus, in the view of some critics, often hold up the action, for example; and the verse in The Two Gentlemen of Verona has been described as stilted.

However, Shakespeare soon began to adapt the traditional styles to his own purposes. The opening soliloquy of Richard III has its roots in the self-declaration of Vice in medieval drama. At the same time, Richard's vivid self-awareness looks forward to the soliloquies of Shakespeare's mature plays. No single play marks a change from the traditional to the freer style. Shakespeare combined the two throughout his career, with Romeo and Juliet perhaps the best example of the mixing of the styles. By the time of Romeo and Juliet, Richard II, and A Midsummer Night's Dream in the mid-1590s, Shakespeare had begun to write a more natural poetry. He increasingly tuned his metaphors and images to the needs of the drama itself.

Shakespeare's standard poetic form was blank verse, composed in iambic pentameter. In practice, this meant that his verse was usually unrhymed and consisted of ten syllables to a line, spoken with a stress on every second syllable. The blank verse of his early plays is quite different from that of his later ones. It is often beautiful, but its sentences tend to start, pause, and finish at the end of lines, with the risk of monotony. Once Shakespeare mastered traditional blank verse, he began to interrupt and vary its flow. This technique releases the new power and flexibility of the poetry in plays such as Julius Caesar and Hamlet. Shakespeare uses it, for example, to convey the turmoil in Hamlet's mind:

Sir, in my heart there was a kind of fighting

That would not let me sleep. Methought I lay

Worse than the mutines in the bilboes. Rashly—

And prais'd be rashness for it—let us know

Our indiscretion sometimes serves us well ...

—Hamlet, Act 5, Scene 2, 4–8

After Hamlet, Shakespeare varied his poetic style further, particularly in the more emotional passages of the late tragedies. The literary critic A. C. Bradley described this style as "more concentrated, rapid, varied, and, in construction, less regular, not seldom twisted or elliptical". In the last phase of his career, Shakespeare adopted many techniques to achieve these effects. These included run-on lines, irregular pauses and stops, and extreme variations in sentence structure and length. In Macbeth, for example, the language darts from one unrelated metaphor or simile to another: "was the hope drunk/ Wherein you dressed yourself?" (1.7.35–38); "... pity, like a naked new-born babe/ Striding the blast, or heaven's cherubim, hors'd/ Upon the sightless couriers of the air ..." (1.7.21–25). The listener is challenged to complete the sense. The late romances, with their shifts in time and surprising turns of plot, inspired a last poetic style in which long and short sentences are set against one another, clauses are piled up, subject and object are reversed, and words are omitted, creating an effect of spontaneity.

Shakespeare combined poetic genius with a practical sense of the theatre. Like all playwrights of the time, he dramatised stories from sources such as Plutarch and Holinshed. He reshaped each plot to create several centres of interest and to show as many sides of a narrative to the audience as possible. This strength of design ensures that a Shakespeare play can survive translation, cutting and wide interpretation without loss to its core drama. As Shakespeare's mastery grew, he gave his characters clearer and more varied motivations and distinctive patterns of speech. He preserved aspects of his earlier style in the later plays, however. In Shakespeare's late romances, he deliberately returned to a more artificial style, which emphasised the illusion of theatre.

Influence

Shakespeare's work has made a lasting impression on later theatre and literature. In particular, he expanded the dramatic potential of characterisation, plot, language, and genre. Until Romeo and Juliet, for example, romance had not been viewed as a worthy topic for tragedy. Soliloquies had been used mainly to convey information about characters or events, but Shakespeare used them to explore characters' minds. His work heavily influenced later poetry. The Romantic poets attempted to revive Shakespearean verse drama, though with little success. Critic George Steiner described all English verse dramas from Coleridge to Tennyson as "feeble variations on Shakespearean themes."

Shakespeare influenced novelists such as Thomas Hardy, William Faulkner, and Charles Dickens. The American novelist Herman Melville's soliloquies owe much to Shakespeare; his Captain Ahab in Moby-Dick is a classic tragic hero, inspired by King Lear. Scholars have identified 20,000 pieces of music linked to Shakespeare's works. These include three operas by Giuseppe Verdi, Macbeth, Otello and Falstaff, whose critical standing compares with that of the source plays. Shakespeare has also inspired many painters, including the Romantics and the Pre-Raphaelites. The Swiss Romantic artist Henry Fuseli, a friend of William Blake, even translated Macbeth into German. The psychoanalyst Sigmund Freud drew on Shakespearean psychology, in particular, that of Hamlet, for his theories of human nature.

In Shakespeare's day, English grammar, spelling, and pronunciation were less standardised than they are now, and his use of language helped shape modern English. Samuel Johnson quoted him more often than any other author in his A Dictionary of the English Language, the first serious work of its type. Expressions such as "with bated breath" (Merchant of Venice) and "a foregone conclusion" (Othello) have found their way into everyday English speech.

Works

Classification of the plays

Shakespeare's works include the 36 plays printed in the First Folio of 1623, listed according to their folio classification as comedies, histories, and tragedies. Two plays not included in the First Folio, The Two Noble Kinsmen and Pericles, Prince of Tyre, are now accepted as part of the canon, with today's scholars agreeing that Shakespeare made major contributions to the writing of both. No Shakespearean poems were included in the First Folio.

In the late 19th century, Edward Dowden classified four of the late comedies as romances, and though many scholars prefer to call them tragicomedies, Dowden's term is often used. In 1896, Frederick S. Boas coined the term "problem plays" to describe four plays: All's Well That Ends Well, Measure for Measure, Troilus and Cressida, and Hamlet. "Dramas as singular in theme and temper cannot be strictly called comedies or tragedies", he wrote. "We may, therefore, borrow a convenient phrase from the theatre of today and class them together as Shakespeare's problem plays." The term, much debated and sometimes applied to other plays, remains in use, though Hamlet is definitively classed as a tragedy. (Source: Wikipedia)

CPSIA information can be obtained
at www.ICGtesting.com
Printed in the USA
BVHW032029020619
549944BV00004B/30/P